② KINGDOM LIVING

THE KEYS TO TRANSFORMATION

All Scripture quotations, unless otherwise indicated, are taken from the Holy Bible, New International Version®, NIV®. Copyright ©1973, 1978, 1984, 2011 by Biblica, Inc.™ Used by permission of Zondervan. All rights reserved worldwide. www.zondervan.com. The "NIV" and "New International Version" are trademarks registered in the United States Patent and Trademark Office by Biblica, Inc.™

Scripture quotations marked NLT are taken from the Holy Bible, New Living Translation, copyright ©1996, 2004, 2015 by Tyndale House Foundation. Used by permission of Tyndale House Publishers, Inc., Carol Stream, Illinois 60188. All rights reserved.

Scripture quotations marked ESV are taken from the ESV® Bible (The Holy Bible, English Standard Version®), copyright © 2001 by Crossway, a publishing ministry of Good News Publishers. Used by permission. All rights reserved.

Scripture taken marked NKJV from the New King James Version®. Copyright © 1982 by Thomas Nelson. Used by permission. All rights reserved.

DESIGN & EDITING:
Anj Marie Riffel, Kingdom Heart Publishing
kingdomheartpublishing.com

KINGDOM LIVING 2: THE KEYS TO TRANSFORMATION
Copyright © 2019. All rights reserved.
Printed in the United States of America.

For information on bulk orders of

KINGDOM LIVING 1: OPENING THE DOOR TO A NEW LIFE
KINGDOM LIVING 2: THE KEYS TO TRANSFORMATION

contact us at info@integratethefaith.com
or order additional copies directly at www.amazon.com

Applying what you believe to every area of life

integratethefaith.com

WELCOME BACK

The Kingdom Living series was developed by a team of people who are passionate about helping you discover your part in God's purpose for the world. Because this book builds on and continues themes from the first book, we recommend that you go through Kingdom Living 1, before proceeding with Kingdom Living 2.

As before, we suggest that you embark on this journey with a friend (or a few friends) so you'll be able to discuss the material as you go. You might even gather with the same group you were with for Kingdom Living 1 to continue deepening those relationships. If you prefer reading this on your own, that's fine too. Either way, please feel free to reach out to us at info@integratethefaith.com with any questions. We're here for you. Additional resources are also available at integratethefaith.com.

Kingdom Living 2 is designed to introduce you to the transformative work of the Holy Spirit in your life. We share the following hope and prayer for you:

> *He [Christ] is the one we proclaim...,*
> *teaching everyone with all wisdom, so that we may*
> *present everyone fully mature in Christ.*
> *— Colossians 1:28*

 INTRODUCTION

Transformed individuals bring transformation to the world. As we learned in Kingdom Living 1, God's perfect creation was corrupted through the actions of an individual man and woman, Adam and Eve. Restoration was made possible through the death and resurrection of another man, Jesus Christ. This restoration is carried out in history through those who are being transformed in every area of their lives — including their beliefs, thoughts, and actions.

The divine metamorphosis God orchestrates takes us from being influenced by evil spiritual forces through our own self-centered desires to being governed by His Spirit. As we yield to the Lord and apply His word in our lives, we become people who are capable of taking part in His larger purposes.

In this second volume of Kingdom Living, you will gain valuable wisdom about participating in God's work of transformation. Chapter 1 lays a foundation for understanding the goal of being Spirit-governed, and describes the process the Lord uses to progressively transform us. The remaining chapters highlight several keys that God has given us for experiencing transformation — the word of God, prayer, faith, and the vitally important topic of living in community with others.

These truths are not intended to remain in a book, or even in your mind. As you apply them to your life, you will become the man or woman God created you to be — an effective agent of transformation in the world.

CONTENTS

WEEK 1: Transformation 11
THE SPIRIT-GOVERNED LIFE
- DAY 1: Growing Up 12
- DAY 2: Spirit, Soul & Body 14
- DAY 3: The Battle 16
- DAY 4: The Process of Transformation 18
- DAY 5: Out with the Old 20
- DAY 6: In with the New 22
- DAY 7: Pruning for a Purpose 24

WEEK 2: The Word of God 27
RESTORING OUR SOULS
- DAY 1: The Source 28
- DAY 2: Ultimate Authority 30
- DAY 3: Take Root, Bear Fruit 32
- DAY 4: Word with Benefits 34
- DAY 5: Take Action 36
- DAY 6: Transforming the World 38
- DAY 7: Abiding 40

WEEK 3: Prayer 43
SHAPING US AND OUR WORLD
- DAY 1: Seated with Christ 44
- DAY 2: Agreeing with God 46
- DAY 3: The Lord's Prayer 48
- DAY 4: Confident Prayer 50
- DAY 5: Open Access 52
- DAY 6: Ongoing Prayer 54
- DAY 7: Practice the Presence 56

WEEK 4:	Faith..59
	PATHWAY TO A PREFERRED FUTURE
	DAY 1: What is Faith?..60
	DAY 2: The Fight of Faith..62
	DAY 3: Increasing Your Faith..64
	DAY 4: Using Your Faith..66
	DAY 5: Faith in Action...68
	DAY 6: Patient Endurance..70
	DAY 7: Entering His Rest..72

WEEK 5:	Community..75
	THE TRANSFORMING POWER OF RELATIONSHIPS
	DAY 1: A Family Environment..76
	DAY 2: Growing Together..78
	DAY 3: Get in the Boat...80
	DAY 4: We Over Me..82
	DAY 5: Extending Reconciliation......................................84
	DAY 6: Relationship Essentials...88
	DAY 7: Love is from God..90

Appendix..93

WEEK 1

Transformation

THE SPIRIT-GOVERNED LIFE

Those who are led by the Spirit of God are sons of God...
The creation waits in eager expectation
for the sons of God to be revealed.
— Romans 8:14,19

 **WEEK 1 / DAY 1 – REVEAL**
GROWING UP

YOU WERE BORN INTO GOD'S FAMILY when you became a follower of Jesus (John 3:3). What an astounding and humbling honor! And this is just the beginning of our Father's intentions for us.

Then we will no longer be infants, tossed back and forth by the waves, and blown here and there by every wind of teaching and by the cunning and craftiness of people in their deceitful scheming. Instead, speaking the truth in love, we will grow to become in every respect the mature body of him who is the head, that is, Christ. — Ephesians 4:14-15

Why is it important for us to grow up?

_____

_____

_____

Every good father and mother wants their kids to develop into their full potential. God's heart is like this, too. He is continually shaping you into the person He created you to be.

When born again by God's Spirit, you were made new — like an infant. How tremendous! This kicks off an amazing time of discovering new things about God, your new identity, His kingdom, and your place in it.

But God does not want you to be an infant forever. He wants you to grow. Our spiritual life mirrors our physical life. We start out as infants, grow as children, develop as young adults, and then become parents. When you follow Jesus as His disciple, your development will follow a similar pattern.

WEEK 1 | DAY 1

STAGES & CHARACTERISTICS OF SPIRITUAL GROWTH*

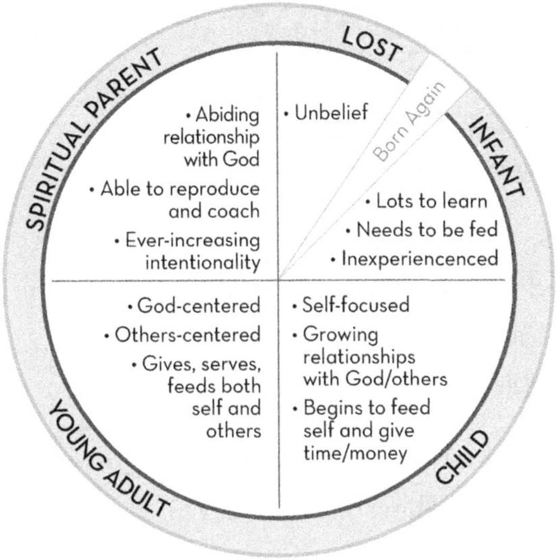

SPIRITUAL PARENT
- Abiding relationship with God
- Able to reproduce and coach
- Ever-increasing intentionality

LOST
- Unbelief

Born Again

INFANT
- Lots to learn
- Needs to be fed
- Inexperienced

YOUNG ADULT
- God-centered
- Others-centered
- Gives, serves, feeds both self and others

CHILD
- Self-focused
- Growing relationships with God/others
- Begins to feed self and give time/money

* Graphic concept courtesy of *Real-Life Discipleship Training Manual*

Which stage of spiritual growth do you currently identify with most? What characteristics do you see in yourself?

_____

_____

_____

You have been birthed into His family. Now it's time to grow! What does that look like? How do we change to increasingly become the people God calls us to be?

This week, we will be looking at the ongoing process God uses to transform us — often called sanctification. *(See Appendix A for working definitions of important terms used and described throughout Kingdom Living 2.)*

Write a prayer asking God to prepare your heart for what He wants to reveal as you go through this book. List any areas that you know He wants to expand or transform in you. Note anything significant that comes to your heart and mind during this time with God.

_____

_____

_____

_____

_____

_____

We pray that you sense the great hope and calling God has for your life as you embrace Him and His desire to see you become everything He made you to be!

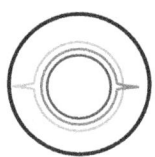

WEEK 1 / DAY 2 – RECEIVE
SPIRIT, SOUL & BODY

Use the Scriptures provided to answer the questions below. <u>Underline</u> the basis for your answers in the margin.

THROUGH THE CROSS, God's redemptive grace rescues us from slavery to sin and then continues to transform every area of our lives. Understanding the way we are made helps us actively participate in this process.

1. What three parts does each person have? What does God desire to do with these? (1 Thessalonians 5:23)

_____

_____

_____

People have a spirit, a soul, and a body. Our body is our physical frame. Our soul is made up of our mind, will, and emotions. Our spirit is the energizing part of us that directly connects with God's Spirit. The biblical word for spirit means wind or breath.

2. When did Adam become a living being? (Genesis 2:7)

_____

1 THESSALONIANS 5:23

²³ May God himself, the God of peace, sanctify you through and through. May your whole spirit, soul and body be kept blameless at the coming of our Lord Jesus Christ.

GENESIS 2:7

⁷ Then the LORD God formed a man from the dust of the ground and breathed into his nostrils the breath of life, and the man became a living being.

BEFORE THE FALL, Adam's spirit, soul, and body were pure, and were united with God's Spirit. Man's thoughts, emotions, and decisions were governed by His spirit.

AFTER SIN entered the world, people came under the enemy's influence and became spiritually dead. In our fallen state, we overly rely on our disordered emotions, intellect, and desires because our spirits are in need of rebirth.

WHEN WE BELIEVE IN JESUS, our spirits are made new and become united with God's Spirit. This union is so close that, when biblical writers use the word "spirit," it is often difficult to tell if they are talking about God's Spirit or our renewed spirit. Although our spirits come alive when we turn to Christ, our souls and bodies are not immediately transformed. Instead, they continue trying to rule our lives. The Bible calls these old thought patterns, desires, habits, and ways of trying to get what we want "the flesh."

As Jesus said: *"Watch and pray so that you will not fall into temptation. The spirit is willing, but the flesh is weak."* — Matthew 26:41

3. If you are a follower of Jesus, what has happened to your spirit? What does this mean for us?

_____

_____

4. What part(s) of you still need(s) transformation? What evidence do you see of this?

_____

_____

God's plan is for your body, soul, and spirit to all be transformed, and for you to be fully re-integrated into the person He intends you to be.

WEEK 1 / DAY 3 – REFLECT & RESPOND
THE BATTLE

THROUGHOUT HIS WRITINGS, the Apostle Paul stressed the fact that we are in a spiritual battle. We get a glimpse of his own inner battle in Romans 7 and 8:

For I do not understand my own actions. For I do not do what I want, but I do the very thing I hate. Now if I do what I do not want, I agree with the law, that it is good. So now it is no longer I who do it, but sin that dwells within me. For I know that nothing good dwells in me, that is, in my flesh. For I have the desire to do what is right, but not the ability to carry it out. For I do not do the good I want, but the evil I do not want is what I keep on doing. Now if I do what I do not want, it is no longer I who do it, but sin that dwells within me.

So I find it to be a law that when I want to do right, evil lies close at hand. For I delight in the law of God, in my inner being, but I see in my members another law waging war against the law of my mind and making me captive to the law of sin that dwells in my members. Wretched man that I am! Who will deliver me from this body of death? Thanks be to God through Jesus Christ our Lord! So then, I myself serve the law of God with my mind, but with my flesh I serve the law of sin. — Romans 7:14-25 (ESV)

What does Paul say about his flesh? What does he say about his inner being?

_____

_____

Do you find yourself having similar struggles as Paul? How?

_____

⁵Those who live according to the flesh have their minds set on what the flesh desires; but those who live in accordance with the Spirit have their minds set on what the Spirit desires. ⁶The mind governed by the flesh is death, but the mind governed by the Spirit is life and peace. ⁷The mind governed by the flesh is hostile to God; it does not submit to God's law, nor can it do so. ⁸Those who are in the realm of the flesh cannot please God.

⁹You, however, are not in the realm of the flesh but are in the realm of the Spirit, if indeed the Spirit of God lives in you. And if anyone does not have the Spirit of Christ, they do not belong to Christ. ¹⁰But if Christ is in you, then even though your body is subject to death because of sin, the Spirit gives life because of righteousness. ¹¹And if the Spirit of him who raised Jesus from the dead is living in you, he who raised Christ from the dead will also give life to your mortal bodies because of his Spirit who lives in you.

¹²Therefore, brothers and sisters, we have an obligation—but it is not to the flesh, to live according to it. ¹³For if you live according to the flesh, you will die; but if by the Spirit you put to death the misdeeds of the body, you will live.

¹⁴For those who are led by the Spirit of God are the children of God. ¹⁵The Spirit you received does not make you slaves, so that you live in fear again; rather, the Spirit you received brought about your adoption to sonship. And by him we cry, "Abba, Father." ¹⁶The Spirit himself testifies with our spirit that we are God's children. — Rom. 8:5-16

List the differences between a mind set on/governed by the flesh verses the Spirit? How does this show up in your own life. Provide any relevant examples. (Romans 8:5-7)

_____
_____
_____
_____

What is the state of our spirit if Christ is in us? What will God's Spirit do to our bodies? What does this mean for your daily life? (Romans 8:10-11)

_____
_____
_____

How are we to deal with the deeds of our flesh? Give an example of how you might face temptation based on these truths. (Romans 8:12-13)

_____
_____
_____

BODY & SOUL

SPIRIT — By living according to the Spirit, body & soul can be transformed.

David prayed that his whole being would be united to honor God's name (Psalm 86:11). Our goal is to grow in the ability to live in accordance with the Spirit, continually bringing every part of our lives under His leadership. As He governs our souls, they are renewed, and we are changed into the people God intends us to be.

In your own words, ask God for victory in the battle against your flesh. Ask Him to show you ways to actively participate in His ongoing transformation and write any insights here.

_____
_____
_____
_____
_____

Therefore, my dear friends, as you have always obeyed... continue to work out your salvation with fear and trembling, for it is God who works in you to will and to act according to his good purpose. — Philippians 2:12-13

WEEK 1 / DAY 4 – RECEIVE
THE PROCESS OF TRANSFORMATION

PSALM 42:1-2
¹As the deer pants for streams of water, so my soul pants for you, my God. ²My soul thirsts for God, for the living God. When can I go and meet with God?

PSALM 27:4,7-8
⁴One thing I ask from the LORD, this only do I seek: that I may dwell in the house of the LORD, all the days of my life, to gaze on the beauty of the LORD and to seek him in his temple. ⁷Hear my voice when I call, LORD; be merciful to me and answer me. ⁸My heart says of you, "Seek his face!" Your face, LORD, I will seek.

PSALM 119:81
⁸¹My soul faints with longing for your salvation, but I have put my hope in your word.

PROVERBS 27:7
⁷One who is full loathes honey from the comb, but to the hungry even what is bitter tastes sweet.

MATTHEW 5:6
⁶"Blessed are those who hunger and thirst for righteousness, for they will be filled."

Use the Scriptures provided to answer the questions below. <u>Underline</u> the basis for your answers in the margin.

OUR LEVEL OF OUR SPIRITUAL HUNGER is crucial in the process of transformation. Are we hungry for God and all He has for us, or are we content with where we currently are?

1. How did the writer of Psalm 42 describe the condition of his soul? (Psalm 42:1-2)

_____

_____

2. What did David long for, hope in, and seek? (Psalm 27:4,7-8; Psalm 119:81)

_____

_____

3. What can prevent us from valuing the things of God? What can help us appreciate even the difficult truths and experiences He leads us into? (Proverbs 27:7)

_____

_____

4. What do you think it means to hunger and thirst for righteousness? (Matthew 5:6)

_____

_____

When we are spiritually hungry, we are eager to experience and hear from God. Not only that, but we also develop an increasing willingness to embrace everything He has for us, even when it is uncomfortable.

GOING DEEPER

God is willing to reveal Himself and His purpose to us. We can experience as much of Him as we want! We can be changed by Him as much as we want! This happens as we sincerely seek Him and align our hearts, our minds, and our wills with His.

In other words, Christ followers must decide over and over again if we value and trust Him enough to lay aside our own desires and plans for something better.

Then He said to them all: "If anyone would come after me, he must deny himself and take up his cross daily and follow me. For whoever wants to save his life will lose it, but whoever loses his life for me will save it." — Luke 9:23-24

It is the cross of Christ — not our own effort — that changes us. Yet, we do have a part to play in this ongoing process. He calls us to continually crucify our flesh by choosing to deny our self-interests and own way of doing things, and instead offering up our lives for God's interests.

If you are ready, pause for a moment right now and pray this simple prayer: "Lord, grow my spiritual hunger for you and your word. I pursue you above everything else, and I fully embrace the transformation process that you are leading me into. Amen."

If you affirmed your desire for God's way over your own way as you prayed that prayer from your heart, something important happened. Be ready to experience more of Him than you could ever imagine!

Use the space below to record any thoughts you would like to remember:

_____
_____
_____
_____

For additional resources visit integratethefaith.com

WEEK 1 / DAY 5 – REFLECT & RESPOND
OUT WITH THE OLD

WHEN SOMEONE MAKES A SACRIFICE, they are giving up something they are attached to because they value someone or something else even more. In the same way, we are to offer every part of our lives to God, even though our flesh desperately wants to remain in charge.

That, however, is not the way of life you learned when you heard about Christ and were taught in him in accordance with the truth that is in Jesus. You were taught, with regard to your former way of life, to put off your old self, which is being corrupted by its deceitful desires; to be made new in the attitude of your minds; and to put on the new self, created to be like God in true righteousness and holiness. — Ephesians 4:20-24

What's wrong with our old nature? What are we to do with it? What must be renewed? What might "out with the old" look like for you?

Therefore, I urge you, brothers and sisters, in view of God's mercy, to offer your bodies as a living sacrifice, holy and pleasing to God—this is your true and proper worship. Do not conform to the pattern of this world, but be transformed by the renewing of your mind. Then you will be able to test and approve what God's will is—his good, pleasing and perfect will. — Romans 12:1-2

What are we to offer to God? Why do you think this is important?

What does it mean to conform to the pattern of this world? Why might this hinder you?

As our minds are being renewed, what will we be able to do? How could this benefit your life?

GOING DEEPER

Before following Christ, we may have lived years or even decades with sinful patterns in our lives. These can become what the Bible calls "strongholds" — false beliefs and ungodly habits we vigorously defend which give our enemy clout. Strongholds are composed of thoughts, attitudes, beliefs, or actions that do not reflect God's character. They are detrimental to our spiritual growth and must be demolished (2 Corinthians 10:3-5).

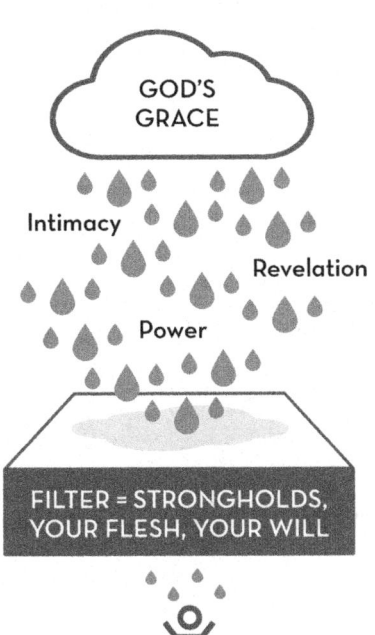

Built up over time, strongholds can block what God desires for us. Imagine Him pouring out grace like water. When our strongholds and our flesh get in the way, His intimacy, power, and revelation do not freely flow to us.

In order to experience life/freedom more fully and become an agent of change for the kingdom, we have to look at what God offers and what we might be holding onto that's actually holding us back.

When you think about God's "good, pleasing and perfect will" for your future, what comes to mind? What do you see yourself doing?

_____
_____
_____

What general areas in your life do you see that get in the way of walking out and living in God's good, pleasing, and perfect will for your life? (e.g., insecurity, fear, pride, control, passivity, lust, bitterness, rejection, etc.) Ask God to show you what lie(s) you have been believing.

_____
_____

If you've identified strongholds today, here's how to deal with them intentionally:
1. Name the stronghold; 2. Repent (change your thinking based on new understanding); 3. Ask God to break its power; 4. Replace the lies that stronghold produced with His truth.

If you're going through this book with someone, it would be great to do this together. Also, continue this process every time the old lies emerge.

Rejection is one common stronghold. See Appendix B for a guide on Reversing the Rejection Cycle.

KINGDOM LIVING 2

WEEK 1 / DAY 6 – RECEIVE
IN WITH THE NEW

2 PETER 1:3-7 (NLT)
³ By his divine power, God has given us everything we need for living a godly life. We have received all of this by coming to know him, the one who called us to himself by means of his marvelous glory and excellence. ⁴ And because of his glory and excellence, he has given us great and precious promises. These are the promises that enable you to share his divine nature and escape the world's corruption caused by human desires.

⁵ In view of all this, make every effort to respond to God's promises. Supplement your faith with a generous provision of moral excellence, and moral excellence with knowledge, ⁶ and knowledge with self-control, and self-control with patient endurance, and patient endurance with godliness, ⁷ and godliness with brotherly affection, and brotherly affection with love for everyone.

1 PETER 1:13-16
¹³ Therefore, with minds that are alert and fully sober, set your hope on the grace to be brought to you when Jesus Christ is revealed at his coming. ¹⁴ As obedient children, do not conform to the evil desires you had when you lived in ignorance. ¹⁵ But just as he who called you is holy, so be holy in all you do; ¹⁶ for it is written: "Be holy, because I am holy."

Use the Scriptures provided to answer the questions below. <u>Underline</u> the basis for your answers in the margin.

WHEN YOU'RE SPIRIT-GOVERNED you'll begin to notice completely changed attitudes and actions in every area of your life. God is passionate about both our CHARACTER and our RELATIONSHIPS.

CHARACTER

1. What do we need in order to live a godly life? (2 Peter 1:3-4)

_____

2. What does Peter instruct us to add to our faith? (2 Peter 1:5-7)

_____
_____

3. What are your biggest temptations? Are there any "triggers" to those temptations? Are you addicted to anything?

_____
_____

4. How much media (including social media) do you consume in a given week? What you do spend your time watching? How is this affecting you?

_____
_____

These are bold questions about our character that require honest examination. God expects that of us (see 1 Peter 1:13-16). To experience transformation, we must be truthful about WHERE WE'RE AT! Living in the freedom that Christ provides does not require immediate perfection, but you should see progress. Allow God to lead you to repentance and holiness!

RELATIONSHIPS

Our character is demonstrated not only in our private lives, but also — and especially — in the way we interact with others. God is very interested in transforming our relationships.

5. What is the second most important commandment? (Matthew 22:36-40)

6. What does growing in Christ-like character lead to? (1 Pet. 1:22)

7. According to Ephesians 5:3, what is improper for God's people? Identify any of these areas that may be a struggle for you. If you're in a romantic relationship, are you honoring God and the other person (especially in the area of sexual purity)?

8. In Ephesians 4:30-32, Paul lists several relational sins. Identify those you may struggle with in any of your relationships.

9. If there are areas in your character or relationships that need attention, how will you cooperate with the Lord to change these attitudes and actions?

Experiencing transformation in our character and relationships is a lifelong process. This is just an introduction. We'll delve deeper tomorrow and again in Week 5.

MATTHEW 22:36-40

[36] "Teacher, which is the greatest commandment in the Law?" [37] Jesus replied: "'Love the Lord your God with all your heart and with all your soul and with all your mind. [38] This is the first and greatest commandment. [39] And the second is like it: 'Love your neighbor as yourself.' [40] All the Law and the Prophets hang on these two commandments."

1 PETER 1:22

[22] Now that you have purified yourselves by obeying the truth so that you have sincere love for each other, love one another deeply, from the heart.

EPHESIANS 5:3

But among you there must not be even a hint of sexual immorality, or of any kind of impurity, or of greed, because these are improper for God's holy people.

EPHESIANS 4:30-32

[30] And do not grieve the Holy Spirit of God, with whom you were sealed for the day of redemption. [31] Get rid of all bitterness, rage and anger, brawling and slander, along with every form of malice. [32] Be kind and compassionate to one another, forgiving each other, just as in Christ God forgave you.

WEEK 1 / DAY 7 - REST
PRUNING FOR A PURPOSE

BEING MADE NEW in our thoughts, attitudes, and actions involves the daily choices we make. Yet the process of transformation is not only about our choices. Our Father is actively involved our growth process.

Consider the following words Jesus spoke to His disciples:

"I am the true vine, and my Father is the gardener. He cuts off every branch in me that bears no fruit, while every branch that does bear fruit he prunes so that it will be even more fruitful."— John 15:1-2

What does the Father do with those who are living fruitful lives? Why?

_____

_____

The pruning process requires cutting away parts of the branch so that the plant's energy will go toward producing more fruit. As the ultimate gardener, God lovingly prunes us, cutting away things that keep us from living fruitful lives for Him. This may involve dealing with how we spend our time, how we treat people, the way we think, and/or our habits.

Pruning is a form of discipline, or training. Just as a gardener prunes a tree so that it grows in the right direction and produces fruit, God trains us so that our lives are focused and effective. He may use difficult circumstances, suffering, input from others, or the conviction of the Holy Spirit to prune us. Pruning, discipline, and training don't usually feel fun! But they have an important purpose.

No discipline seems pleasant at the time, but painful. Later on, however, it produces a harvest of righteousness and peace for those who have been trained by it. — Hebrews 12:11

Though it may hurt sometimes, God is working to bring about His character in our lives. His discipline allows us to experience His righteousness and peace. It causes us to live focused and useful lives for His kingdom.

Now that you understand the overall process of becoming Spirit-led, you can actively participate with the Father in His work of transformation. Don't run from this process, but embrace it. Your life will never be the same, and you will become the person God designed you to be. The following chapters will discuss some of the powerful means God has given us to bring about the increase of His government in our lives and the world around us.

Today, get in a quiet, private place and spend time thanking God for the transformation He has brought about in your heart and life so far. Write down the big ones that come to mind. Allow the fact that God is fighting for you and working actively in your life to wash over you. Pray that He would open your eyes to what He has done in and through you since you began following Him.

Write your reflections here:

WEEK 2

The Word of God

RESTORING OUR SOULS

*The law of the LORD is perfect, restoring the soul;
the testimony of the LORD is sure, making wise the simple.
The precepts of the LORD are right, rejoicing the heart
the commandment of the LORD is pure, enlightening the eyes...
The judgments of the LORD are true; they are righteous altogether.
They are more desirable than gold, yes, than much fine gold;
Sweeter also than honey and the drippings of the honeycomb.
Moreover, by them Your servant is warned;
In keeping them there is great reward.*

— Psalm 19:7-11 (NAS)

WEEK 2 / DAY 1 – REVEAL
THE SOURCE

In the beginning was the Word... — John 1:1

AT THE BEGINNING of creation God spoke the words, "Let there be light," and there was light. He created the universe and everything it contains by speaking it into existence (see Genesis 1:3-26). He didn't wave a magic wand or simply think creative thoughts — He spoke! The word of God is behind everything we can see.

In the same way, God's word has dynamic power to take us beyond what we can otherwise experience or accomplish. It can transform our lives and environments, no matter what problems or challenges we face.

Consider Christ's perspective on the importance of God's word in our lives:

Jesus answered, "It is written: 'Man shall not live on bread alone, but on every word that comes from the mouth of God.'" — Matthew 4:44

What do you think this means?

_____

_____

_____

A proper diet is essential for physical health. Failing to eat right makes us weak, lethargic, and prone to getting sick. A person who stops eating will soon die. If we want to be emotionally and spiritually healthy, and if we want to grow and be transformed, we need to regularly and consistently "eat" God's word by receiving, understanding, and applying it.

Every powerful person of faith possesses a hunger for God's word. The prophet Jeremiah described it like this:

When your words came, I ate them; they were my joy and my heart's delight, for I bear your name, LORD God Almighty. — Jeremiah 15:16

Have you experienced this in your own life? If so, how? How might you experience more of this joy and delight?

___

Write a prayer asking God to...

- help you understand how His word brings transformation.

- increase your appreciation and hunger for His word.

- help you develop daily habits of hearing, learning, and applying His word.

___

WEEK 2 / DAY 2 – RECEIVE
ULTIMATE AUTHORITY

Use the Scriptures provided to answer the questions below. <u>Underline</u> the basis for your answers in the margin.

HEBREWS 1:3 (ESV)
³ He [the Son] is the radiance of the glory of God and the exact imprint of his nature, and he upholds the universe by the word of his power.

1. What does Jesus do by His word? (Hebrews 1:3)
_____

MATTHEW 24:35
³⁵ "Heaven and earth will pass away, but my words will never pass away."

2. How long will His words be in effect? (Mat. 24:35, Isaiah 40:8)
_____

ISAIAH 40:8
⁸ "The grass withers and the flowers fall, but the word of our God endures forever."

3. The word is _____. What does it do in us? (Jn. 17:17)
_____

JOHN 17:17 (ESV)
¹⁷ "Sanctify them in the truth; your word is truth."

The Bible is God's word to humankind. When we read, hear, study and meditate on the Scripture, God reveals to us more of who He is, tells us how to live, and sanctifies/transforms us.

2 PETER 1:20-21
²⁰ Above all, you must understand that no prophecy of Scripture came about by the prophet's own interpretation of things. ²¹ For prophecy never had its origin in the human will, but prophets, though human, spoke from God as they were carried along by the Holy Spirit.

4. From where does Scripture originate? (2 Pet. 1:20-21, 2 Tim. 3:16)
_____
_____
_____

5. What are the Scriptures useful for? (2 Timothy 3:16-17)
_____

2 TIMOTHY 3:16-17 (ESV)
¹⁶ All Scripture is breathed out by God and profitable for teaching, for reproof, for correction, and for training in righteousness, ¹⁷ that the man of God may be complete, equipped for every good work.
_____
_____

6. What will our lives ultimately be judged by? (John 12:48)
_____

JOHN 12:48
⁴⁸ "There is a judge for the one who rejects me and does not accept my words; the very words I have spoken will condemn them at the last day."

God's words reflect His righteousness and goodness. His promises, commands, and instructions have the power to change us. When we understand and apply God's word to our lives and in our culture, it changes things from the way they are to the way He intends them to be.

Along with providing nourishment, God's word also confronts and convicts us. This is essential if we are to experience transformation from our old ways of thinking and living.

7. Describe the word of God. What does it do? (Hebrews 4:12-13)

_____

_____

If we are going to be transformed, the word of God must do its work in our hearts and minds. When we hear God's word, it shows us where we have been thinking our own thoughts and going our own way. It tells us how God is calling us to live, and how we need to be changed.

God's word first brings revelation — showing us what is true. Then it transforms the way we think. Ultimately, it changes the way we live as we follow God's commands and apply His teaching in our lives.

8. How does Christ make the Church holy? (Ephesians 5:25-27)

_____

_____

9. How are our souls transformed (saved)? (James 1:21)

_____

_____

10. What are we instructed to let Christ's word do? (Col. 3:16)

_____

_____

It's not enough to merely hear the word. We are to "let it dwell in us richly." This happens as we read, listen to, ponder, speak, and even sing it. Then, as we hear and understand the word of God, we are to obey it.

HEBREWS 4:12-13 (NAS)
[12] For the word of God is living and active and sharper than any two-edged sword, and piercing as far as the division of soul and spirit, of both joints and marrow, and able to judge the thoughts and intentions of the heart. [13] And there is no creature hidden from His sight, but all things are open and laid bare to the eyes of Him with whom we have to do.

EPHESIANS 5:25-27 (NLT)
[25] For husbands, this means love your wives, just as Christ loved the church. He gave up his life for her [26] to make her holy and clean, washed by the cleansing of God's word. [27] He did this to present her to himself as a glorious church without a spot or wrinkle or any other blemish. Instead, she will be holy and without fault.

JAMES 1:21
[21] Therefore, get rid of all moral filth and the evil that is so prevalent and humbly accept the word planted in you, which can save you.

COLOSSIANS 3:16 (ESV)
[16] Let the word of Christ dwell in you richly, teaching and admonishing one another in all wisdom, singing psalms and hymns and spiritual songs, with thankfulness in your hearts to God.

WEEK 2 / DAY 3 – REFLECT & RESPOND
TAKE ROOT, BEAR FRUIT

TO ILLUSTRATE THE POTENTIAL of God's word to bring about great results in our lives — and to warn us about what can hinder this process — Jesus told a parable about a farmer who sowed seed on different kinds of soil.

Read Mark 4:1-20 in your Bible.

In this story, what does the seed represent? (Mark 4:14) _____

On what four types of soil did the seed fall?

1. _____ 2. _____
3. _____ 4. _____

What happened to the seed in each situation? Why?

The hard path: _____
The rocky soil: _____
The thorny ground: _____
The good soil: _____

To become the people God has called us to be, we must be like the good soil, receiving God's word and letting it grow in our hearts. However, various obstacles can prevent this from happening.

What's your number one excuse that keeps you from getting in the word?

_____

What's the truth about this excuse?

_____

WEEK 2 | DAY 3

🔎 GOING DEEPER

You can get the word of God inside you many different ways. It is important to think about (meditate on) what you are reading, and it is often impactful to speak (confess) God's word out loud. You can also listen to preaching (live or recorded), or an audio version of the Bible.

To develop the essential daily habit of reading the Bible, first, find a time and a place where you can be undistracted and fully engaged. Then, engage with God personally.

One tried-and-true pattern for doing this is called S.O.A.P. (Scripture, Observe, Apply, Pray):

S   Choose a passage of <u>Scripture</u> (for this exercise, let's use the entire chapter of Mark 4). Before you begin, ask God to speak something specific to you. Read slowly and jot down a key verse or passage that stands out.

_____

_____

O   <u>Observe</u> what God is showing you. Any truths or principles to learn or remember? What is the overall message for you?

_____

_____

A   How does this <u>Apply</u> to your life? Any encouragement you need to believe and hold onto? Any instruction to obey?

_____

_____

P   <u>Pray</u> in response. Ask God to help you use this truth, or ask for greater insight. Write a prayer, then pray it. As you do, listen to what He is saying to you.

_____

_____

Hopefully you were able to go deeper and connect the Scripture with your own life by reading Mark 4 again with this method. The goal is to hear personally from God as He speaks to you, teaches you His ways, and leads you to follow Him more fully. Establishing this pattern will make all the difference in the world. After completing Kingdom Living 2, you'll want to get a new notebook for this practice.

For more detail, check out the S.O.A.P. video on integratethefaith.com

KINGDOM LIVING 2

WEEK 2 / DAY 4 – RECEIVE
WORD WITH BENEFITS

PSALM 19:7-11 (NAS)
⁷ The law of the LORD is perfect, restoring the soul; The testimony of the LORD is sure, making wise the simple. ⁸ The precepts of the LORD are right, rejoicing the heart; The commandment of the LORD is pure, enlightening the eyes. ⁹ The fear of the LORD is clean, enduring forever; The judgments of the LORD are true; they are righteous altogether. ¹⁰ They are more desirable than gold, yes, than much fine gold; Sweeter also than honey and the drippings of the honeycomb. ¹¹ Moreover, by them Your servant is warned; In keeping them there is great reward.

PSALM 1:1-3
¹ Blessed is the one who does not walk in step with the wicked or stand in the way that sinners take or sit in the company of mockers, ² but whose delight is in the law of the LORD, and who meditates on his law day and night. ³ That person is like a tree planted by streams of water, which yields its fruit in season and whose leaf does not wither— whatever they do prospers.

JOHN 8:31-32
³¹ To the Jews who had believed him, Jesus said, "If you hold to my teaching, you are really my disciples. ³² Then you will know the truth, and the truth will set you free."

Use the Scriptures provided to answer the questions below. <u>Underline</u> the basis for your answers in the margin.

GOD CALLED DAVID a "man after my own heart" (Acts 13:22). His friendship with the Lord led him to becoming one of the most influential songwriters and leaders ever. For David, loving God was inseparable from delighting in, learning, and following His written word.

1. What benefits of God's commandments did David appreciate? (Psalm 19:7-8)

_____

_____

2. What can keep us from pursuing God's word? (Psalm 1:1)

_____

3. Describe the person who meditates on God's word. (Psalm 1:2-3)

_____

_____

4. What do true disciples do? What is the result? (John 8:31-32)

_____

5. What was God's command to Joshua? What did He promise if Joshua obeyed? (Joshua 1:7-9, see page 35)

Command: _____

_____

Promise: _____

_____

6. What do you think it means to "keep this Book… always on your lips; meditate on it day and night?" (Joshua 1:8)

7. Why do you think Joshua needed strength and courage? Do you need strength and courage to follow Christ? Why? (Joshua 1:7,9)

8. How did Jesus overcome temptation? (Matthew 4:8-11)

9. How can a Christian live blamelessly and walk in victory over sin? (Psalm 119:1-3, 9-11)

10. List some of the other ways God's word benefits us. (Psalm 119:98, 105)

11. As a result, how did the Psalmist approach Scripture? (Psalm 119:147-148)

WEEK 2 | DAY 4

JOSHUA 1:7-9
[7] "Be strong and very courageous. Be careful to obey all the law my servant Moses gave you; do not turn from it to the right or to the left, that you may be successful wherever you go. [8] Keep this Book of the Law always on your lips; meditate on it day and night, so that you may be careful to do everything written in it. Then you will be prosperous and successful." [9] "Have I not commanded you? Be strong and courageous. Do not be afraid; do not be discouraged, for the LORD your God will be with you wherever you go."

MATTHEW 4:8-11
[8] Again, the devil took him to a very high mountain and showed him all the kingdoms of the world and their splendor. [9] "All this I will give you," he said, "if you will bow down and worship me." [10] Jesus said to him, "Away from me, Satan! For it is written: 'Worship the Lord your God, and serve him only.'" [11] Then the devil left him, and angels came and attended him.

PSALM 119:1-3, 9-11, 97-98, 105, 147-148
[1] Blessed are those whose ways are blameless, who walk according to the law of the LORD. [2] Blessed are those who keep his statutes and seek him with all their heart— [3] they do no wrong but follow his ways. … [9] How can a young person stay on the path of purity? By living according to your word. [10] I seek you with all my heart; do not let me stray from your commands. [11] I have hidden your word in my heart that I might not sin against you…. [97] Oh, how I love your law! I meditate on it all day long. [98] Your commands are always with me and make me wiser than my enemies…. [105] Your word is a lamp for my feet, a light on my path…. [147] I rise before dawn and cry for help; I have put my hope in your word. [148] My eyes stay open through the watches of the night, that I may meditate on your promises.

WEEK 2 / DAY 5 - REFLECT & RESPOND
TAKE ACTION

TO BE TRANSFORMED and experience blessing, we must first hear the word of God and let it take root in our hearts. But hearing is just the starting point. Jesus put it this way:

"Why do you call me, 'Lord, Lord,' and do not do what I say? As for everyone who comes to me and hears my words and puts them into practice, I will show you what they are like. They are like a man building a house, who dug down deep and laid the foundation on rock. When a flood came, the torrent struck that house but could not shake it, because it was well built. But the one who hears my words and does not put them into practice is like a man who built a house on the ground without a foundation. The moment the torrent struck that house, it collapsed and its destruction was complete." — Luke 6:46-49

If we call Jesus our Lord, what should we do? What else in this story stands out?

_____
_____

Where have you experienced "collapse and destruction" from doing things your own way?

_____
_____

What is one teaching of Jesus you have put into practice? What were the benefits?

_____
_____
_____
_____

🔍 GOING DEEPER

Living under Christ's Lordship is a prior decision to obey everything God tells us to believe and do. If Jesus is our Lord, we do not decide if we will obey Him based on whether we like, agree, or even understand His instructions. If His word clearly commands it, then our love toward Him is lived out in active, trusting obedience:

Do not merely listen to the word, and so deceive yourselves. Do what it says. Anyone who listens to the word but does not do what it says is like someone who looks at his face in a mirror and, after looking at himself, goes away and immediately forgets what he looks like. But whoever looks intently into the perfect law that gives freedom, and continues in it—not forgetting what they have heard, but doing it — they will be blessed in what they do. — James 1:22-25

What are we like if we only listen to the word without acting on it?
What happens when we apply God's word in our lives?

_____
_____

It's always a challenge when God's will contradicts ours! This often happens when He asks us to sacrifice our own desires or because we don't know how obeying Him will work out.

How about you? Are you willing to obey everything God commands? Even when it crosses your own will? What if it seems impossible?

Write your reflections below. If you're ready, write or say a prayer committing to pursue God's will as He has revealed it in the Bible, and to apply it in every area of your life.

_____
_____
_____
_____
_____

For additional resources visit integratethefaith.com

WEEK 2 / DAY 6 - RECEIVE
TRANSFORMING THE WORLD

MATTHEW 28:18-20
¹⁸ Then Jesus came to them and said, "All authority in heaven and on earth has been given to me. ¹⁹ Therefore go and make disciples of all nations, baptizing them in the name of the Father and of the Son and of the Holy Spirit, ²⁰ and teaching them to obey everything I have commanded you."

DEUTERONOMY 28:1-14
¹ "If you fully obey the LORD your God and carefully follow all his commands I give you today, the LORD your God will set you high above all the nations on earth. ² All these blessings will come on you and accompany you if you obey the LORD your God: ³ You will be blessed in the city and blessed in the country. ⁴ The fruit of your womb will be blessed, and the crops of your land and the young of your livestock—the calves of your herds and the lambs of your flocks. ⁵ Your basket and your kneading trough will be blessed. ⁶ You will be blessed when you come in and blessed when you go out. ⁷ The LORD will grant that the enemies who rise up against you will be defeated before you. They will come at you from one direction but flee from you in seven. ⁸ The LORD will send a blessing on your barns and on everything you put your hand to. The LORD your God will bless you in the land he is giving you. ⁹ "The LORD will establish you as his holy people, as he promised you on oath, if you keep the commands of the LORD your God and walk in obedience to him.

Use the Scriptures provided to answer the questions below. <u>Underline</u> the basis for your answers in the margin.

GOD IS INTENT on bringing His kingdom into the world. His Word tells us how things should look in our interactions with others — and in every area of culture.

1. What did Jesus tell his followers to do with the nations? (Matthew 28:19)

_____

2. What are we to teach them? (Matthew 28:20)

_____

Our instructions are to disciple every nation. While we tend to read the Bible through individualistic eyes, God is concerned with how whole communities should function. His word speaks to the practical affairs of cities and nations.

The Bible addresses issues of education, gender, sexual conduct, marriage, and parenting. It provides guidelines for economics and the workplace. God has much to say about racism, the role of civil government, crime, agricultural practices and the stewardship of natural resources, and more. In His word, God gives instruction that will help bring His good reign into every area of life. It's our responsibility to search out and apply these commands in the areas of our individual calling.

3. What did God promise to the nation of Israel if they carefully followed His commands? (Deuteronomy 28:1-14)

v. 2-3 _____

v. 4 _____

v. 6 _____

v. 7 _____

v. 8 _____

v. 9-10 _____

v. 11 _____

v. 12 _____

v. 13 _____

4. What did God warn would happen if they did not follow His commands? (Deuteronomy 28:15-20, 25)

_____

_____

_____

God's word tells us how to live and build our communities. Blessings follow when we obey His commands. If we go our own way, we suffer. God's word will always serve as a blueprint for how society should operate. It's important to recognize that God has called us to extend His kingdom into the world by learning the truths of His word, then exercising responsibility and influence everywhere we go.

DEUT. 28:1-14 continued
[10] Then all the peoples on earth will see that you are called by the name of the LORD, and they will fear you. [11] The LORD will grant you abundant prosperity—in the fruit of your womb, the young of your livestock and the crops of your ground—in the land he swore to your ancestors to give you. [12] The LORD will open the heavens, the storehouse of his bounty, to send rain on your land in season and to bless all the work of your hands. You will lend to many nations but will borrow from none. [13] The LORD will make you the head, not the tail. If you pay attention to the commands of the LORD your God that I give you this day and carefully follow them, you will always be at the top, never at the bottom. [14] Do not turn aside from any of the commands I give you today, to the right or to the left, following other gods and serving them."

DEUT. 28:15-20, 25
[15] "However, if you do not obey the LORD your God and do not carefully follow all his commands and decrees I am giving you today, all these curses will come on you and overtake you: [16] You will be cursed in the city and cursed in the country. [17] Your basket and your kneading trough will be cursed. [18] The fruit of your womb will be cursed, and the crops of your land, and the calves of your herds and the lambs of your flocks. 19 You will be cursed when you come in and cursed when you go out. [20] The LORD will send on you curses, confusion and rebuke in everything you put your hand to, until you are destroyed and come to sudden ruin because of the evil you have done in forsaking him....[25] The LORD will cause you to be defeated before your enemies."

WEEK 2 / DAY 7 - REST
ABIDING

WELL DONE — you've persevered to the end of another transformative week! This is a good time to practice abiding in God by drawing near to Him and receiving life from His words.

Read John 15 in your own Bible, and S.O.A.P. it:

S   Scripture

O   Observe

A   Apply

P   Pray

A key to establishing most habits is finding a regular time and place to practice them. Studying God's word is no different. Don't let distractions, worries, and the busyness of life crowd out the Word. Have you instilled this pattern in your daily routine yet? What habit do you want to begin from this point forward?

 GOING DEEPER

This week we focused on learning and applying God's word. Transformation happens when we become devoted to routinely "eating the word" in the same way that you eat regular meals. Finding a daily time (or times) and place to meet with God, get in the Word, and pray is invaluable to your health and growth.

The following spiritual exercises will help you get the most from God's word:

KEEP A NOTEBOOK – Do S.O.A.P. Write down what God speaks to you and your response.

DECLARE THE WORD – Speak God's word out loud while thinking about what you are saying and actively believing it.*

> *"Do not let this Book of the Law depart from your mouth..."* — Joshua 1:8

MEMORIZE SCRIPTURE – Commit passages of the Bible to memory.*

> *I have hidden your word in my heart that I might not sin against you.* — Psalm 119:11

READ THROUGH THE BIBLE – You can go through the Bible in one year by reading one chapter in the New Testament, two or three chapters in the Old Testament and a Psalm each day. We recommend the Read Scripture app from the Bible Project.*

> *The sum of Your word is truth, and every one of your righteous ordinances is everlasting.* — Psalm 119:160 (NAS)

PREACHING – Take notes during messages at church, then go over them during the week.

> *...in humility receive the word implanted, which is able to save your souls.* — James 1:21 (NAS)

> *Now the Berean Jews were of more noble character than those in Thessalonica, for they received the message with great eagerness and examined the Scriptures every day to see if what Paul said was true.* — Acts 17:11

SHARE IT – Passing on what you're learning and proclaiming the Gospel to others will motivate you and help you internalize the word like nothing else!

> *Like cold water to a weary soul is good news from a distant land.* — Proverbs 25:25

Choose one of these, and start today! If you're going through this book with others, ask for encouragement and accountability in the new habits you're instilling.

*See Appendix E for Scriptures to actively declare. For additional Scriptures and resources visit integratethefaith.com

WEEK 3

Prayer

SHAPING US & OUR WORLD

"This, then is how you should pray:
'Our Father in heaven, hallowed be Your name. Your kingdom come, Your will be done, on earth as it is in heaven.'"
— Matthew 6:9-10

WEEK 3 / DAY 1 - REVEAL
SEATED WITH CHRIST

Therefore he is able to save completely those who come to God through him, because he always lives to intercede for them. — Hebrews 7:25

PRAYER IS SO IMPORTANT that Jesus is praying (interceding) for you right now! Prayer has the power to transform us and our world. But first, the way we think about prayer must be transformed.

Our natural tendency is to view God as someone who is far off. In addition, we frequently feel as if we are unworthy to approach Him. We are often unsure if our prayers even get through, much less get answered. At the same time, many of us feel guilty for not praying more!

Prayer can be as simple as talking to God, just as you would a friend — but it has profound results. Transformational prayer begins with understanding the access we've been given to God.

And God raised us up with Christ and seated us with him in the heavenly realms in Christ Jesus... — Ephesians 2:6

Where has God placed us? Is it difficult for you to believe this is true? If so, why?

Let us then approach God's throne of grace with confidence, so that we may receive mercy and find grace to help us in our time of need. — Hebrews 4:16

How are we to come before God? What are the implications of this?

From our position with Christ, we can have our hearts moved by the things that move Him and listen to the counsel the Father gives us. Then, with both our words and actions, we can agree with heaven and change the shape of history.

Think about a time when you've felt close to God. What did it feel like to sense His presence? If applicable, describe how this impacted your perspective when praying.

_____

_____

_____

What's one area of the world that needs change?

_____

_____

Write a prayer
- asking God what His perspective is about this situation.
- asking Him what He wants you to do about it.
- asking Him to do what only He can do.

_____

_____

_____

_____

_____

_____

_____

_____

_____

WEEK 3 / DAY 2 - RECEIVE
AGREEING WITH GOD

JOHN 10:27 (NAS)
²⁷ "My sheep hear my voice, and I know them, and they follow me."

JOHN 15:7-16 (NAS)
⁷ "If you abide in Me, and My words abide in you, ask whatever you wish, and it will be done for you. ⁸ My Father is glorified by this, that you bear much fruit, and so prove to be My disciples. ⁹ Just as the Father has loved Me, I have also loved you; abide in My love. ¹⁰ If you keep My commandments, you will abide in My love; just as I have kept My Father's commandments and abide in His love. ¹¹ These things I have spoken to you so that My joy may be in you, and that your joy may be made full."
¹² "This is My commandment, that you love one another, just as I have loved you. ¹³ Greater love has no one than this, that one lay down his life for his friends. ¹⁴ You are My friends if you do what I command you. ¹⁵ No longer do I call you slaves, for the slave does not know what his master is doing; but I have called you friends, for all things that I have heard from My Father I have made known to you. ¹⁶ You did not choose Me but I chose you, and appointed you that you would go and bear fruit, and that your fruit would remain, so that whatever you ask of the Father in My name He may give to you. ¹⁷ This I command you, that you love one another."

Use the Scriptures provided to answer the questions below. <u>Underline</u> the basis for your answers in the margin.

KNOWING GOD
You get to know someone by spending time with them and conversing together. The same is true with God. He invites us to confidently enter His presence. There, we interact with Him through prayer and come to know Him personally.

1. Jesus calls those who believe, His flock. How does He describe His interaction with us? (John 10:27)

___

Read John 15:7-16

2. What did Jesus say is required for us to have our prayers answered? (John 15:7)

___

3. How do we abide in His love? (John 15:10,12)

___

4. What is a benefit of being a friend of God? (John 15:15)

___

5. What does Jesus promise His disciples? (John 15:16)

___

What an awesome privilege it is to be a friend of God! Through prayer, our friendship with Him grows.

WEEK 3 | DAY 2

KNOWING GOD'S WILL

It's easy to be overly focused on ourselves. God invites us to zero in on much more. He's ready to let us know what He desires, and what He's planning. When we put kingdom priorities and the good of others above our own desires, we are drawn into a closer friendship and partnership with God.

6. Before Jesus acted or spoke, what did He do? (John 8:28, John 5:19-20)

7. Who did Jesus seek to please? (John 5:30) _____

Jesus is a model of someone completely in tune with the Father's agenda. In a similar way, as we prayerfully read the Bible and listen to God, He brings us into His council — inviting us to be active participants in carrying out His will.

8. What kind of prayer can we be confident God hears and answers? (1 John 5:14-15)

9. What stands out to you from Paul's prayer for the Colossian church? (Colossians 1:9-12)

Much of God's will is revealed to us in Scripture. For example, we can confidently pray for such things as: for His kingdom to come around us, and for people to encounter Him.

When we consult with the Lord, He gives us insight about how we are to deal with specific situations. He provides creativity and new ideas. After receiving our directives, we can agree with God, and then join Him in what He is leading us into.

Pray Col. 1:9-12 — for yourself and another person/group.

JOHN 8:28 (NAS)
Jesus said, "I do nothing on My own initiative, but I speak these things as the Father taught Me."

JOHN 5:19-20
[19] Jesus gave them this answer: "Very truly I tell you, the Son can do nothing by himself; he can do only what he sees his Father doing, because whatever the Father does the Son also does. [20] For the Father loves the Son and shows him all he does. Yes, and he will show him even greater works than these, so that you will be amazed."

JOHN 5:30
[30] "By myself I can do nothing; I judge only as I hear, and my judgment is just, for I seek not to please myself but him who sent me."

1 JOHN 5:14-15
[14] This is the confidence we have in approaching God: that if we ask anything according to his will, he hears us. [15] And if we know that he hears us—whatever we ask—we know that we have what we asked of him.

COLOSSIANS 1:9-12
[9] For this reason, since the day we heard about you, we have not stopped praying for you. We continually ask God to fill you with the knowledge of his will through all the wisdom and understanding that the Spirit gives, [10] so that you may live a life worthy of the Lord and please him in every way: bearing fruit in every good work, growing in the knowledge of God, [11] being strengthened with all power according to his glorious might so that you may have great endurance and patience, [12] and giving joyful thanks to the Father, who has qualified you to share in the inheritance of his holy people in the kingdom of light.

WEEK 3 / DAY 3 – REFLECT
THE LORD'S PRAYER

PEOPLE WERE ASTONISHED at the way Jesus modeled a relationship with the Father. The closeness He had with God and the way He lived and ministered to others was completely different from other religious teachers. Curious to learn how to pray like their leader, the disciples asked Jesus how to go about it. Here's His reply:

"This, then, is how you should pray: '"Our Father in heaven, hallowed be your name, your kingdom come, your will be done, on earth as it is in heaven. Give us today our daily bread. And forgive us our debts, as we also have forgiven our debtors. And lead us not into temptation, but deliver us from the evil one. For Yours is the kingdom and the power and the glory forever. Amen.'" — Matthew 6:9-13

This powerful prayer is often called "the Lord's Prayer." Using this model as a blueprint is an outstanding way to come before God and pray. It provides a perfect grid to follow and apply personally to the situations we are dealing with and trusting Him in.

Try it for yourself! The table on the next page will help you take each element of the Lord's Prayer deeper by specifically applying it to your life and the world around you.

WEEK 3 | DAY 3

 GOING DEEPER

Fill in each box below with something personal, then bring these requests directly to our Father.

Our Father in heaven, hallowed be Your name,	Choose an aspect of God's character from today's reading:	
Your kingdom come, Your will be done, On earth as it is in heaven.	My church/ministry arena:	
	Church/ministry to pray for:	
	Seekers to pray for:	
	Social issue or nation to pray for:	
Give us today Our daily bread.	Details of my day:	
	Financial need:	
	My family:	
	People to pray for:	
And forgive us our debts, as we also have forgiven our debtors. And lead us not into temptation, But deliver us from the evil one.	Confession:	
	People I need to forgive:	
	Areas where I need discipline/protection:	
For yours is the kingdom and the power and the glory forever. Amen.	Attitude/situation to yield to His Lordship	

Downloadable and printable PDF's of this guide are available at integratethefaith.com.

KINGDOM LIVING 2

WEEK 3 / DAY 4 – RECEIVE
CONFIDENT PRAYER

Use the Scriptures provided to answer the questions below. <u>Underline</u> the basis for your answers in the margin.

OUR OPEN ACCESS to God offers great confidence. We are seated with Christ and His blood cleanses us from all sin. We have a covenant with God and the authority to do His work. As we live to please Him, we can expect Him to answer our prayers.

1. What attitude can believers have before God? (1 John 3:21-22)

_____

2. What did Jesus say He would do when we ask for things in his name? Why? (John 14:13)

_____

Praying in Jesus' name is not like reciting a magic formula — as if we will get whatever we want simply because our prayer ends with a certain phrase. Instead, this means to pray in His authority. This comes from being connected with Him and praying in agreement with His will (Matthew 6:9-10).

Incorporating Scripture is a good way to do this — whether a Psalm, a biblical prayer, or another passage. (That's why the "P" for "Pray" is part of S.O.A.P.) The Holy Spirit will often help you by bringing phrases from the Bible to your mind as you pray.

3. The prayer of a righteous person is _____ and _____. (James 5:16)

4. What happens when someone prays in faith without doubting? (Mark 11:22-24)

_____

5. What confidence can we have about our prayers? Why? (Matthew 7:7-11)

_____
_____

---

1 JOHN 3:21-22 (NAS)
²¹ Beloved, if our heart does not condemn us, we have confidence before God; ²² and whatever we ask we receive from Him, because we keep His commandments and do the things that are pleasing in His sight.

JOHN 14:13
¹³ "And I will do whatever you ask in my name, so that the Father may be glorified in the Son. ¹⁴ You may ask me for anything in my name, and I will do it."

MATTHEW 6:9-10 (NAS)
"Pray, then, in this way… your kingdom come, your will be done, on earth as it is in heaven."

JAMES 5:16
¹⁶ …The prayer of a righteous person is powerful and effective.

MARK 11:22-24
²² "Have faith in God," Jesus answered. ²³ "Truly I tell you, if anyone says to this mountain, 'Go, throw yourself into the sea,' and does not doubt in their heart but believes that what they say will happen, it will be done for them. ²⁴ Therefore I tell you, whatever you ask for in prayer, believe that you have received it, and it will be yours."

MATTHEW 7:7-11
⁷ "Ask and it will be given to you; seek and you will find; knock and the door will be opened to you. ⁸ For everyone who asks receives; the one who seeks finds; and to the one who knocks, the door will be opened. ⁹ "Which of you, if your son asks for bread, will give him a stone? ¹⁰ Or if he asks for a fish, will give him a snake? ¹¹ If you, then, though you are evil, know how to give good gifts to your children, how much more will your Father in heaven give good gifts to those who ask him!"

MATTHEW 18:19-20 (NAS)
"Again I say to you, that if two of you agree on earth about anything that they may ask, it shall be done for them by my Father who is in heaven. For where two or three have gathered together in my name, I am there in their midst."

6. What happens when we gather with other believers and pray in agreement? (Matthew 18:19-20, see previous page)

_____
_____

Whether in person, over the phone, or in a prayer meeting, joining with others boosts our prayers even more! Pay attention to what others are praying and agree in your heart and with your words.

7. Who can you pray with this week? When?

_____

FASTING, abstaining from food or other things to prioritize time with God, can increase the effectiveness of our prayer life.

8. What is the purpose of fasting? (Isaiah 58:6)

_____

9. What else results from praying and fasting in secret? (Matthew 6:17-18)

_____

10. Have you ever fasted? If so, what was your experience like? Did anything extraordinary happen?

_____
_____

To learn more, check out resources about fasting at integratethefaith.com.

11. What can hinder our prayers?

Psalm 66:18-19 _____

Mark 11:25-26 _____

James 1:5-8 _____

James 4:2-3 _____

1 Peter 3:7 _____

Our prayers will be impeded by sin and any areas of our lives that are not honoring to the Lord. On the other hand, God honors and answers our prayers when we are aligned with Him and His ways.

ISAIAH 58:6
[6] "Is not this the kind of fasting I have chosen: to loose the chains of injustice and untie the cords of the yoke, to set the oppressed free and break every yoke?"

MATTHEW 6:17-18
[17] "But when you fast, put oil on your head and wash your face, [18] so that it will not be obvious to others that you are fasting, but only to your Father, who is unseen; and your Father, who sees what is done in secret, will reward you."

PSALM 66:18-19
[18] If I had cherished sin in my heart, the Lord would not have listened; [19] but God has surely listened and has heard my prayer.

MARK 11:25
[25] And when you stand praying, if you hold anything against anyone, forgive them, so that your Father in heaven may forgive you your sins."

JAMES 1:5-8
[5] If any of you lacks wisdom, you should ask God, who gives generously to all without finding fault, and it will be given to you. [6] But when you ask, you must believe and not doubt, because the one who doubts is like a wave of the sea, blown and tossed by the wind. [7] That person should not expect to receive anything from the Lord. [8] Such a person is double-minded and unstable in all they do.

JAMES 4:2-3
[2] You desire but do not have, so you kill. You covet but you cannot get what you want, so you quarrel and fight. You do not have because you do not ask God. [3] When you ask, you do not receive, because you ask with wrong motives, that you may spend what you get on your pleasures.

1 PETER 3:7
[7] Husbands, in the same way be considerate as you live with your wives, and treat them with respect as the weaker partner and as heirs with you of the gracious gift of life, so that nothing will hinder your prayers.

WEEK 3 / DAY 5 – REFLECT & RESPOND
OPEN ACCESS

PRAYER can be one of the most thrilling things we do. Think about it — when you take time to be in prayer, you are communing with the God of all creation! Because of His grace and great love for us, He hears us and speaks to us. May we never lose sight of just how awesome this privilege is.

Many think of prayer as a one-way monologue. But it's really a two-way conversation.

"My sheep listen to my voice; I know them, and they follow me." — John 10:27

As we follow Jesus, we should expect to hear God's guiding voice. Learning to recognize His voice doesn't usually happen overnight. It takes practice. Start by asking the Lord simple, answerable questions. Some good questions might be:

- Lord, how do you see me?
- Lord, what is on your heart for me today?
- Are there any areas of disobedience in my life?
- Is there one of my brothers or sisters in Christ who needs encouragement? If so, what would you like me to say?
- Lord, what is your heart for the church community I'm involved with?
- What is on your heart for the world today?

Pick one or two of these questions and get to a quiet place. In prayer, ask a question and wait to hear God speak to your heart.

Write down what you hear. *(Remember: God's voice is loving, encouraging, and convicting — but never condemning.)*

 GOING DEEPER

Let's do another exercise. Another way the Lord can speak to us is through images. Below are two portions of Scripture that describe what it's like to come before the Lord in prayer.

As you read, allow God to paint a picture in your imagination and personalize the scene:
Shout for joy to the LORD, all the earth. Worship the LORD with gladness; come before him with joyful songs. Know that the LORD is God. It is he who made us, and we are his; we are his people, the sheep of his pasture. Enter his gates with thanksgiving and his courts with praise; give thanks to him and praise his name. For the LORD is good and his love endures forever; his faithfulness continues through all generations. — Psalm 100:1-5

Now, interact with God as you see yourself before Him in prayer.

What images came to mind as you read this passage?

_____
_____
_____

What emotions came to the surface as you put yourself in these verses?

_____
_____

Let's do the same thing with a New Testament passage — visualize as you read:

Therefore, since we have a great high priest who has ascended into heaven, Jesus the Son of God, let us hold firmly to the faith we profess. For we do not have a high priest who is unable to empathize with our weaknesses, but we have one who has been tempted in every way, just as we are—yet he did not sin. Let us then approach God's throne of grace with confidence, so that we may receive mercy and find grace to help us in our time of need. - Hebrews 4:14-16

Allow the Spirit to paint a mental picture as you "approach His throne of grace with confidence."

If this were a scene (like in a movie), how would you describe it?

_____
_____
_____
_____

For additional resources visit integratethefaith.com

WEEK 3 / DAY 6 – RECEIVE
ONGOING PRAYER

THESSALONIANS 5:16-18
16 Rejoice always, 17 pray continually, 18 give thanks in all circumstances; for this is God's will for you in Christ Jesus.

EPHESIANS 6:18-20
18 And pray in the Spirit on all occasions with all kinds of prayers and requests. With this in mind, be alert and always keep on praying for all the Lord's people. 19 Pray also for me, that whenever I speak, words may be given me so that I will fearlessly make known the mystery of the gospel, 20 for which I am an ambassador in chains. Pray that I may declare it fearlessly, as I should.

LUKE 10:1,8-9
1 After this the Lord appointed seventy-two others and sent them two by two ahead of him to every town and place where he was about to go. ... 8 "When you enter a town and are welcomed, eat what is offered to you. 9 Heal the sick who are there and tell them, 'The kingdom of God has come near to you.'"

MATTHEW 10:1,5,7-8
1 Jesus called his twelve disciples to him and gave them authority to drive out impure spirits and to heal every disease and sickness 5 ...with the following instructions: 7..."As you go, proclaim this message: 'The kingdom of heaven has come near.' 8 Heal the sick, raise the dead, cleanse those who have leprosy, drive out demons. Freely you have received; freely give."

Use the Scriptures provided to answer the questions below. <u>Underline</u> the basis for your answers in the margin.

WITHDRAWING FOR FOCUSED PRAYER is important — setting aside time to read the Word and pray is one of the best habits you can instill. But it doesn't end there. We can also be in communication with the Lord as we actively do His will out in the world.

PRAYING AS YOU GO

1. When should we pray? How should we pray? What should we pray for? (1 Thessalonians 5:16-18, Ephesians 6:18-20)

_____
_____
_____

2. Before sending His disciples out on ministry assignments, what did Jesus authorize them to do? (Luke 10:1,8-9, Mat. 10:1,5,7-8)

_____
_____
_____

3. What should we do if we are suffering? Cheerful? Sick? (James 5:13-16, see *following page*)

_____
_____

Like Jesus, you can converse with the Father throughout the day, while actively doing His will. You may find that your prayers become less self-focused and more about meeting the practical and spiritual needs of others.

PRAYING IN THE SPIRIT

4. What do you think it means to pray in the Spirit? (Ephesians 6:18, see previous page)

_____

5. How does the Spirit help us pray? (Romans 8:26-27)

_____

_____

Praying in the Spirit often involves praying in tongues. The Holy Spirit helps us by interceding in a spiritual prayer language — even when we don't know what to say! With this spiritual gift, we can pray for exactly what God wants at any time.

6. Recall the diagrams of our body, soul, and spirit from Week 1, Days 2 - 3. When we pray in tongues, our mind takes a back seat. Can you think of any advantages of this? (1 Cor. 14:14-15)

_____

7. According to 1 Corinthians 14, what happens when we pray in tongues? (v. 3) _____
Is this gift reserved for a select few? (v. 5) _____
Is it to be used sparingly? (v. 18) _____

It's important to pray with both mind and spirit. If you've not yet experienced this gift, you can ask God for it! (1 Corinthians 14:1.)

EXERCISES

- Take a short walk — possibly even just going around your room — and pray as you go. Make a point to keep an ongoing dialogue with the Lord going today.
- This week, pray for someone to experience physical healing.
- The next time you are discouraged, ask God to lift you up.
- Talk to your Kingdom Living 2 friends about how praying continually is going. Ask any questions you have about healing, fasting, praying in the Spirit, or anything else.

JAMES 5:13-16 (NAS)
[13] Is anyone among you suffering? Then he must pray. Is anyone cheerful? He is to sing praises. [14] Is anyone among you sick? Then he must call for the elders of the church and they are to pray over him, anointing him with oil in the name of the Lord; [15] and the prayer offered in faith will restore the one who is sick, and the Lord will raise him up, and if he has committed sins, they will be forgiven him.

ROMANS 8:26-27 (NAS)
[26] In the same way the Spirit also helps our weakness; for we do not know how to pray as we should, but the Spirit Himself intercedes for us with groanings too deep for words; [27] and He who searches the hearts knows what the mind of the Spirit is, because He intercedes for the saints according to the will of God.

1 CORINTHIANS 14:14-15 (NLT)
[14] For if I pray in tongues, my spirit is praying, but I don't understand what I am saying. [15] Well then, what shall I do? I will pray in the spirit, and I will also pray in words I understand. I will sing in the spirit, and I will also sing in words I understand.

1 CORINTHIANS 14:3 (ESV)
[3] The one who speaks in a tongue builds up himself...

1 CORINTHIANS 14:5
[5] I would like every one of you to speak in tongues...

1 CORINTHIANS 14:18
[18] I thank God that I speak in tongues more than all of you.

1 CORINTHIANS 14:1
[1] Follow the way of love and eagerly desire gifts of the Spirit...

# WEEK 3 / DAY 7 – REST
PRACTICE THE PRESENCE

TODAY (AND EVERY DAY!) offers a great opportunity to enjoy God's presence. The following practices are proven ways to nurture your friendship and partnership with God.

1) SOLITUDE AND STILLNESS

We live in a noisy, fast-paced world, and are constantly bombarded with ideas from different sources. It's important to have times of quietness when we simply listen to God.

"Be still, and know that I am God; I will be exalted among the nations, I will be exalted in the earth." – Psalm 46:10

Jesus went deeper in His relationship with the Father through solitude. It's how He began His ministry, made decisions, handled life's demands, and dealt with challenges and grief.

But Jesus often withdrew to lonely places and prayed. – Luke 5:16

After He had sent them away, he went up to the mountain by Himself to pray. When evening came, He was there alone... – Matthew 14:23

Jesus practiced solitude and stillness often. So should we.

2) THANKSGIVING AND PRAISE

The simple act of telling someone thank you or offering a compliment can mean so much. This is even more true – and appropriate – in our relationship with the Lord.

Enter his gates with thanksgiving and his courts with praise; give thanks to him and praise his name. -– Psalm 100:4

Thanking and praising God honors Him, and also leads to breakthroughs for us. It causes our self-centeredness and anxiety to dissipate and reminds us that He's the one we're living for. An attitude of thanksgiving and praise prepares us to hear from God and do His will.

 GOING DEEPER

As Christ's followers, we must pattern our lives after Him. With that in mind, take time now to practice solitude with God.

Go before the Lord in prayer. Allow Him to reshape your perspective, recharge your heart, renew your mind, and refocus your life. Talk to Him about anything — large or small — that comes to mind. Listen to hear anything He wants to speak to your heart.

As you do this, practice thanking and praising God for who He is and what you have been seeing Him do in your life recently. Continue to listen for what He wants to say to you.

Write down what you heard and/or anything that stood out to you during this time of solitude, thanksgiving, and praise:

For additional resources visit integratethefaith.com

WEEK 4

Faith

PATHWAY TO A PREFERRED FUTURE

"For we live by faith, not by sight."
— 2 Corinthians 5:7

WEEK 4 / DAY 1 – REVEAL
WHAT IS FAITH?

HEBREWS 11:1 (NKJV)
¹ Now faith is the substance of things hoped for, the evidence of things not seen.

HEBREWS 11:3
³ By faith we understand that the universe was formed at God's command, so that what is seen was not made out of what was visible.

ROMANS 1:18-20
¹⁸ The wrath of God is being revealed from heaven against all the godlessness and wickedness of people, who suppress the truth by their wickedness, ¹⁹ since what may be known about God is plain to them, because God has made it plain to them. ²⁰ For since the creation of the world God's invisible qualities—his eternal power and divine nature—have been clearly seen, being understood from what has been made, so that people are without excuse.

MATTHEW 16:15-17
¹⁵ "But what about you?" he asked. "Who do you say I am?" ¹⁶ Simon Peter answered, "You are the Messiah, the Son of the living God." ¹⁷ Jesus replied, "Blessed are you, Simon son of Jonah, for this was not revealed to you by flesh and blood, but by my Father in heaven."

Use the Scriptures provided to answer the questions below. <u>Underline</u> the basis for your answers in the margin.

EVIDENCE
People often say, "It can't be proven. You've just got to have faith." However, faith is much more than wishful thinking. It doesn't contradict the truth, but agrees with it.

1. What is the biblical definition of faith? (Hebrews 11:1)

_____

2. How was the universe formed? How do we come to know this? (Hebrews 11:3)

_____

3. What has God made evident to everyone? What do people do with the plain truth about God? (Romans 1:18-20)

_____

4. Who did Peter say Jesus was? How did he know this? (Matthew 16:15-17)

_____

Our unbelief is not caused by a lack of evidence, but by denying the evidence. Faith is believing the truth our Father graciously uncovers for us. And when we act on the faith He gives us, our level of understanding increases.

LENS
Faith is seeing the way God does. We can view things with natural sight or "see" ultimate reality through the lens of faith.

5. What is faith the evidence of? (Hebrews 11:1)

_____

6. What is everything we can physically see made from? (Hebrews 11:3)

_____

7. How do disciples live? (2 Corinthians 5:7)

God's unseen word is behind everything we see. Living by faith is living according to what He says, instead of according to our natural perceptions — or our doubts.

8. What did Thomas say he needed in order to believe Jesus had risen? What did Jesus tell Thomas? (John 20:25-29)

Through the lens of faith, we can trust in God's word instead of listening to our doubts and fears. Instead of our problems, we can look to His promises. And instead of noticing other people's weaknesses, we can see God's purpose for their lives.

UNDERSTANDING

If you don't trust God/the Bible, then you are left to trust your own reasoning/perceptions, the opinions of others, or something else as your source of understanding. Everyone believes *something* — it's a question of what we put our faith in.

9. Who should we trust and why? (Proverbs 3:5-6)

10. Where does faith come from? What do we need to hear? (Romans 10:17)

When the Bible talks about hearing, it often refers to spiritual understanding. As we "listen" to and internalize God's word with a hungry and teachable heart, our understanding and knowledge of Him increases — and so does our faith!

11. How should we pursue understanding? (Proverbs 2:3-5)

Ask God to increase your faith, then watch expectantly!

---

2 CORINTHIANS 5:7
[7] For we live by faith, not by sight.

JOHN 20:25-29
[25] So the other disciples told him [Thomas], "We have seen the Lord!" But he said to them, "Unless I see the nail marks in his hands and put my finger where the nails were, and put my hand into his side, I will not believe." [26] A week later his disciples were in the house again, and Thomas was with them. Though the doors were locked, Jesus came and stood among them and said, "Peace be with you!" [27] Then he said to Thomas, "Put your finger here; see my hands. Reach out your hand and put it into my side. Stop doubting and believe." [28] Thomas said to him, "My Lord and my God!" [29] Then Jesus told him, "Because you have seen me, you have believed; blessed are those who have not seen and yet have believed."

PROVERBS 3:5-6 (ESV)
[5] Trust in the Lord with all your heart, and do not lean on your own understanding. [6] In all your ways acknowledge him, and he will make straight your paths.

ROMANS 10:17 (ESV)
[17] So faith comes from hearing, and hearing through the word of Christ.

PROVERBS 2:3-5
...[3] indeed, if you call out for insight and cry aloud for understanding, [4] and if you look for it as for silver and search for it as for hidden treasure, [5] then you will understand the fear of the LORD and find the knowledge of God.

WEEK 4 / DAY 2 – RECEIVE
THE FIGHT OF FAITH

1 TIMOTHY 6:12
¹² Fight the good fight of the faith. Take hold of the eternal life to which you were called when you made your good confession in the presence of many witnesses.

MATTHEW 11:12 (NIV)
¹² "From the days of John the Baptist until now, the kingdom of heaven has been forcefully advancing, and forceful men lay hold of it."

ROMANS 14:23
²³ ...everything that does not come from faith is sin.

HEBREWS 3:16-19
¹⁶ Who were they who heard and rebelled? Were they not all those Moses led out of Egypt? ¹⁷ And with whom was he angry for forty years? Was it not with those who sinned, whose bodies perished in the wilderness? ¹⁸ And to whom did God swear that they would never enter his rest if not to those who disobeyed? ¹⁹ So we see that they were not able to enter, because of their unbelief.

MATTHEW 28:17
¹⁷ When they saw him, they worshiped him; but some doubted.

Use the Scriptures provided to answer the questions below. <u>Underline</u> the basis for your answers in the margin.

WHEN JESUS was training His disciples, He repeatedly — and sternly — admonished them for their lack of faith. Their unbelief (and the intense way He dealt with it) shows us that living by faith is challenging and of utmost importance — it does not happen without a fight.

1. What is required to experience the life God intends for us? (1 Timothy 6:12)

___

In the battle for our faith, we must face the enemies of unbelief, fear, and anxiety. We are often tempted to look at our circumstances instead of God and His word.

2. According to Jesus, how does the kingdom of God advance? What kind of people receive it? (Matthew 11:12)

___

We cannot win the fight for our faith if we are passive. Instead, we must actively push our enemies aside and lay hold of God's promises.

3. What does the Bible call faithless actions? (Romans 14:23)

___

4. What kept a generation of Israelites from entering their promised land? (Hebrews 3:16-19)

___

5. How did those who saw Jesus after His resurrection respond? What does this tell us? (Matthew 28:17, see *previous page*)

_____
_____
_____

6. What should we worry about? Why? (Matthew 6:25-34)

_____
_____
_____

7. What happens when we lift up our faith against the attacks of our enemy? (Ephesians 6:16)

_____
_____

8. What is the work God has called us to? (John 6:28-29)

_____
_____

The enemy of faith is fear. Doubts and worries try to dominate our thinking, seeking to persuade us that they are the most formidable forces in our lives. To grow in our faith, we must deal with every enemy that tries to undermine it.

When we actively place our trust in Jesus and line up our thoughts, words, and actions with His word, we push back our enemies. Although it is often intense and not finished overnight, the victory we gain will ultimately make the fight worthwhile.

MATTHEW 6:25-34
25 "Therefore I tell you, do not worry about your life, what you will eat or drink; or about your body, what you will wear. Is not life more than food, and the body more than clothes? 26 Look at the birds of the air; they do not sow or reap or store away in barns, and yet your heavenly Father feeds them. Are you not much more valuable than they? 27 Can any one of you by worrying add a single hour to your life]? 28 "And why do you worry about clothes? See how the flowers of the field grow. They do not labor or spin. 29 Yet I tell you that not even Solomon in all his splendor was dressed like one of these. 30 If that is how God clothes the grass of the field, which is here today and tomorrow is thrown into the fire, will he not much more clothe you—you of little faith? 31 So do not worry, saying, 'What shall we eat?' or 'What shall we drink?' or 'What shall we wear?' 32 For the pagans run after all these things, and your heavenly Father knows that you need them. 33 But seek first his kingdom and his righteousness, and all these things will be given to you as well. 34 Therefore do not worry about tomorrow, for tomorrow will worry about itself. Each day has enough trouble of its own."

EPHESIANS 6:16
16 In addition to all this, take up the shield of faith, with which you can extinguish all the flaming arrows of the evil one.

JOHN 6:28-29
28 Then they asked him, "What must we do to do the works God requires?"
29 Jesus answered, "The work of God is this: to believe in the one he has sent."

WEEK 4 / DAY 3 – REFLECT & RESPOND
INCREASING YOUR FAITH

...God has allotted to each a measure of faith. — Romans 12:3

WE ARE ALL GIVEN a "starter's kit" of faith, but it is our responsibility to develop it. One of the marks of someone who is being transformed into a Spirit-led man or woman is that they are growing in their faith.

"I tell you the truth, if you have faith as small as a mustard seed, you can say to this mountain, 'Move from here to there' and it will move. Nothing will be impossible for you." — Matthew 17:20

STARTING SMALL

None of us begin with great faith. However, God can do amazing things through us when we start with just a small amount of faith and act on it.

When the spirit saw Jesus, it immediately threw the boy into a convulsion. He fell to the ground and rolled around, foaming at the mouth. Jesus asked the boy's father, "How long has he been like this?"

"From childhood," he answered. "It has often thrown him into fire or water to kill him. But if you can do anything, take pity on us and help us."

"'If you can'?" said Jesus. "Everything is possible for one who believes."

Immediately the boy's father exclaimed, "I do believe; help me overcome my unbelief!"

When Jesus saw that a crowd was running to the scene, he rebuked the impure spirit. "You deaf and mute spirit," he said, "I command you, come out of him and never enter him again." The spirit shrieked, convulsed him violently and came out. The boy looked so much like a corpse that many said, "He's dead." But Jesus took him by the hand and lifted him to his feet, and he stood up. — Mark 9:20-27

How much faith do you think the man had when he first asked Jesus for help? How did Jesus answer the man? What did Jesus do?

GOING DEEPER

Jesus always meets us where we are, but He doesn't leave us there. Instead, He challenges us to stretch our faith. When we recognize our weakness and ask Him to help increase our faith, He does.

Consider the following words of Jesus:

"Truly, I say to you, unless you turn and become like children, you will never enter the kingdom of heaven. Whoever humbles himself like this child is the greatest in the kingdom of heaven." — Matthew 18:2-4 (ESV)

How must we receive the kingdom of God? What do you think this means?

_____

_____

And by faith even Sarah, who was past childbearing age, was enabled to bear children because she considered him faithful who had made the promise. — Hebrews 11:11

What was the basis for Sarah's faith?

_____

One of the qualities of children is that they trust their parents. In the same way, God is looking for people who consider Him trustworthy and take Him at His word — regardless of circumstances or feelings. When He finds someone with this kind of faith, He comes through in powerful ways.

How would you describe your faith currently? What tends to undercut your faith?

_____

_____

Want to see your faith grow? If so, use the space below to ask God for increased faith. Your faith will grow as you obey Him. What is He calling you to? Is there anything He has been asking you to do that you haven't fully obeyed yet?

_____

_____

_____

Go do it. See how He meets you there — and increases your faith in the process! Share this step of faith/obedience with someone this week.

WEEK 4 / DAY 4 – RECEIVE
USING YOUR FAITH

Use the Scriptures provided to answer the questions below. <u>Underline</u> the basis for your answers in the margin.

KINGDOM FOCUS

1. What can happen as we live by faith? (Hebrews 11:33-35)

_____
_____

HEBREWS 11:33-35
³³ ...who through faith conquered kingdoms, administered justice, and gained what was promised, who shut the mouths of lions, ³⁴ quenched the fury of the flames, and escaped the edge of the sword; whose weakness was turned to strength; and who became powerful in battle and routed foreign armies. ³⁵ Women received back their dead, raised to life again. There were others who were tortured, refusing to be released so that they might gain an even better resurrection.

GENESIS 12:1-3 (ESV)
¹ Now the LORD said to Abram, "Go from your country and your kindred and your father's house to the land that I will show you. ² And I will make of you a great nation, and I will bless you and make your name great, so that you will be a blessing. ³ I will bless those who bless you, and him who dishonors you I will curse, and in you all the families of the earth shall be blessed."

ROMANS 4:13
¹³ It was not through the law that Abraham and his offspring received the promise that he would be heir of the world, but through the righteousness that comes by faith.

HEBREWS 11:10
¹⁰ For he was looking forward to the city with foundations, whose architect and builder is God.

The ultimate purpose of faith is not merely to trust God for personal things, but to advance His rule and reign in the world. One person who modeled this kind of faith is Abraham, the man known as "the father of faith."

2. What did it cost Abraham to follow God? (Genesis 12:1)

_____

3. What did God promise He would do *for* Abraham? What did He promise to do *through* Abraham? (Genesis 12:2-3)

_____
_____

4. What promise has been given to us, as Abraham's offspring? How is it fulfilled? (Romans 4:13)

_____

5. What was Abraham's focus? (Hebrews 11:10)

_____

Abraham realized his greatest blessing was the opportunity to be involved in "the city with foundations" coming to the nations of the earth.

In the same way, God invites us to play a part in the unfolding of His plan: that every corner of the world will experience the blessings of His kingdom.

ABOVE THE CIRCUMSTANCES

God told Abraham that his descendants would be as numerous as sand on a seashore. Yet Abraham was 100 years old before his promised son was born. His wife Sarah was 90 — well past normal child-bearing years! Abraham looked beyond his circumstances and feelings, and put his faith in something greater.

6. Describe Abraham's faith. (Romans 4:16-21)

_____

_____

7. Rather than focus on human limitations, what did Abraham do? Why? (Romans 4:17,21)

_____

_____

Despite the fact that it looked impossible, Abraham did not give up. He believed the promise, because God said it was true. He knew the Lord was able to do what He had promised, no matter what things looked like.

We are called to exercise our faith in the same way. It's easy to look at our circumstances — both in our individual lives and in the world around us — and give up on God's promises. However, when things look impossible, God is able to display His power even more. He is looking for people who will believe His word regardless of what is going on around them.

8. Is there a promise you have heard from God that is not yet fulfilled? If not, ask God for one! If yes, what will it look like for you to "keep faith alive" in this area?

_____

_____

_____

ROMANS 4:16-21

[16] Therefore, the promise comes by faith, so that it may be by grace and may be guaranteed to all Abraham's offspring—not only to those who are of the law but also to those who have the faith of Abraham. He is the father of us all. [17] As it is written: "I have made you a father of many nations." He is our father in the sight of God, in whom he believed—the God who gives life to the dead and calls into being things that were not.

[18] Against all hope, Abraham in hope believed and so became the father of many nations, just as it had been said to him, "So shall your offspring be." [19] Without weakening in his faith, he faced the fact that his body was as good as dead—since he was about a hundred years old—and that Sarah's womb was also dead. [20] Yet he did not waver through unbelief regarding the promise of God, but was strengthened in his faith and gave glory to God, [21] being fully persuaded that God had power to do what he had promised.

WEEK 4 / DAY 5 - REFLECT & RESPOND
FAITH IN ACTION

WHEN WE TRUST GOD, our faith leads us to live in a radically unusual way. We make our time, talent, and treasure available to God and to others. The apostle James described it like this:

What good is it, my brothers and sisters, if someone claims to have faith but has no deeds? Can such faith save them? Suppose a brother or a sister is without clothes and daily food. If one of you says to them, "Go in peace; keep warm and well fed," but does nothing about their physical needs, what good is it? In the same way, faith by itself, if it is not accompanied by action, is dead.

But someone will say, "You have faith; I have deeds."

Show me your faith without deeds, and I will show you my faith by my deeds. You believe that there is one God. Good! Even the demons believe that—and shudder.

You foolish person, do you want evidence that faith without deeds is useless? Was not our father Abraham considered righteous for what he did when he offered his son Isaac on the altar? You see that his faith and his actions were working together, and his faith was made complete by what he did. And the scripture was fulfilled that says, "Abraham believed God, and it was credited to him as righteousness," and he was called God's friend. You see that a person is considered righteous by what they do and not by faith alone.

In the same way, was not even Rahab the prostitute considered righteous for what she did when she gave lodging to the spies and sent them off in a different direction? As the body without the spirit is dead, so faith without deeds is dead. — James 2:14-26

With this passage in mind, what can make putting faith into action a challenge? What are the costs and risks of living with faith? Anything else stand out to you?

_____
_____
_____

What examples of faith in action have you admired in others or acted upon yourself?

_____
_____

 GOING DEEPER

As we can see from what James wrote, faith inevitably involves being radically generous towards God and others. True faith is inconvenient, sacrificial, and risky.

Is your faith working? How about in the following areas: the way you are spending your time, how you are investing your talent (abilities, spiritual gifts), and what you are doing with your treasure (money, home, possessions).

Fundamental ways we trust God with our time and talent include faithfully attending church, being part of a small group, and serving others. A basic and essential starting point of trusting God with our treasure is by tithing — giving the first 10% of our income back to Him. See Appendix D for more on the topic of giving.

Prayerfully consider what God is saying to you today. Are you putting your faith into action with your time, your talent, and your treasure? What inconvenient, sacrificial, and risky steps of faith and obedience is He leading you to take?

	YES/NO	STEP OF FAITH AND OBEDIENCE
TIME	_____	_____
TALENT	_____	_____
TREASURE	_____	_____

If you truly trust God and believe His promises, it will be evident in your everyday actions. As you exercise your faith, you will see Him come through in ways only He can. You will also experience His pleasure, and the blessing of knowing that your life is making a difference.

For additional resources visit integratethefaith.com

KINGDOM LIVING 2

WEEK 4 / DAY 6 – RECEIVE
PATIENT ENDURANCE

Use the Scriptures provided to answer the questions below. <u>Underline</u> the basis for your answers in the margin.

LOOKING AT the world around us, the prevalence of evil is obvious. Is God's kingdom really advancing? It takes faith to recognize what He's doing, and fight the forces of evil, even through tough times.

The promise made to Abraham did not come quickly, either. Long decades passed before he saw the first visible evidence of its fulfillment. During this time, he experienced much hardship and emotional pain. But his faith grew stronger as he patiently endured, holding on to what God had promised.

HEBREWS 6:11-15
¹¹ We want each of you to show this same diligence to the very end, so that what you hope for may be fully realized. ¹² We do not want you to become lazy, but to imitate those who through faith and patience inherit what has been promised. ¹³ When God made his promise to Abraham, since there was no one greater for him to swear by, he swore by himself, ¹⁴ saying, "I will surely bless you and give you many descendants." ¹⁵ And so after waiting patiently, Abraham received what was promised.

1. How is our hope "fully realized?" (Hebrews 6:11-12)

_____

2. What did Abraham have to do to obtain God's promise? (Hebrews 6:15)

_____
_____

LUKE 17:20-21
²⁰ Once, on being asked by the Pharisees when the kingdom of God would come, Jesus replied, "The coming of the kingdom of God is not something that can be observed, ²¹ nor will people say, 'Here it is,' or 'There it is,' because the kingdom of God is in your midst."

The people of Jesus' day expected the Messiah to usher in the kingdom with great fanfare and an overwhelming show of military force that no one could miss. Jesus told them they misunderstood the nature of the kingdom.

3. How is the kingdom different than we expect? (Luke 17:20-21)

_____
_____

JAMES 1:2-4
² Consider it pure joy, my brothers and sisters, whenever you face trials of many kinds, ³ because you know that the testing of your faith produces perseverance. ⁴ Let perseverance finish its work so that you may be mature and complete, not lacking anything.

God's kingdom comes in ways that are not obvious to our natural perceptions. In a broken world, it takes faith see it, even though it is already in our midst. If we are to be part of its expansion, we must be transformed from our old ways of thinking — and patiently endure without losing faith.

4. How should we respond when we face difficulties? Why? (James 1:2-3, see *previous page*)

_____

_____

5. What is the result of having endurance? (James 1:4)

_____

_____

Many of God's greatest promises take time to unfold. If we received everything right away, we would not need much faith. When results do not come quickly, we can either give up, or grow in faith and endurance. Believing in God's ultimate purpose during these challenges gives meaning to our daily lives.

6. Why should we not lose heart? How? (2 Corinthians 4:17)

_____

_____

It's easy to lose sight of the importance of what God has called us to do. Service in the kingdom — whether raising children, loving our neighbors, doing our jobs faithfully, or serving in the church — can seem monotonous and insignificant. But we find joy and strength to continue by realizing our labor is not in vain. God is using it to produce something weighty, lasting, and glorious.

7. What will it look like for you to continue exercising your faith in the ways you listed on Days 4 and 5 of this week?

_____

_____

8. What will you have to overcome if you are to endure in this?

_____

_____

Pray Ephesians 1:15-22 out loud for yourself and your church.

---

2 CORINTHIANS 4:16-18
[16] Therefore we do not lose heart. Though outwardly we are wasting away, yet inwardly we are being renewed day by day. [17] For our light and momentary troubles are achieving for us an eternal glory that far outweighs them all. [18] So we fix our eyes not on what is seen, but on what is unseen, since what is seen is temporary, but what is unseen is eternal.

EPHESIANS 1:15-22
[15] For this reason, ever since I heard about your faith in the Lord Jesus and your love for all God's people, [16] I have not stopped giving thanks for you, remembering you in my prayers. [17] I keep asking that the God of our Lord Jesus Christ, the glorious Father, may give you a spirit of wisdom and revelation, so that you may know him better. [18] I pray that the eyes of your heart may be enlightened in order that you may know the hope to which he has called you, the riches of his glorious inheritance in his holy people, [19] and his incomparably great power for us who believe. That power is the same as the mighty strength [20] he exerted when he raised Christ from the dead and seated him at his right hand in the heavenly realms, [21] far above all rule and authority, power and dominion, and every name that is invoked, not only in the present age but also in the one to come. [22] And God placed all things under his feet and appointed him to be head over everything for the church, [23] which is his body, the fullness of him who fills everything in every way.

WEEK 4 / DAY 7 - REST
ENTERING HIS REST

HEBREWS 3 WARNS of the perils of unbelief and disobedience — the Israelites were not allowed to enter the Promised Land for forty years. We are told to encourage one another daily and hold on to our conviction firmly, so that we might enter God's rest. Hebrews 4 tells us more about this promise.

Read Hebrews 4 in your Bible and practice S.O.A.P. Look especially for the connection between faith and experiencing true rest.

S   Scripture

___

O   Observe

___

A   Apply

___

P   Pray

___

COLLECTIVE FAITH

People of faith experience — and bring about — transformation. In turn, this transformation produces greater faith. Those who are being transformed are always growing in faith. This is especially true when a group of people is believing in unity together, as in the book of Acts:

All the believers were one in heart and mind. — Acts 4:32

Just as cyclists find a place of rest and increased energy by drafting off their team members, our faith grows when we are around other people of faith. And when a group applies their faith to pursue the purposes of God together, they become a force to be reckoned with.

Where this kind of collective faith is present, God's people are extraordinarily empowered. They bring His kingdom not only to individual lives, but to every area of society.

As a group lives with a common vision to see the kingdom come, believing that all things are possible, a powerful culture of faith emerges. People are constantly thinking of new ways to work together to address the needs of the world with kingdom solutions that honor God.

Next week, we will look more closely at how God uses community to produce transformation. Take a minute now to imagine the kind of church community that would most powerfully impact your region. Ask God to bring you into partnership with others in a way that will greatly increase the level of transformation you — and the world around you — are experiencing.

Write the highlights of the community you imagined and your prayer here:

WEEK 5

Community

THE TRANSFORMING POWER OF RELATIONSHIPS

As iron sharpens iron, so one person sharpens another.
— Proverbs 27:17

WEEK 5 / DAY 1 – REVEAL
A FAMILY ENVIRONMENT

The Lord God said, "It is not good for the man to be alone. I will make a helper suitable for him." — Genesis 2:18

AS WE SAW at the end of last week, living by faith is not an individual pursuit. God never designed for us to be alone. He intentionally created us to live in communities that help and work with one another.

Why do you think it's not good for people to be alone?

_____

_____

Genesis 2:15 tells us that God placed man in the Garden of Eden to work and take care of it. God then revealed that it would be good for Adam to find a partner who could help him take care of creation. The first family was formed from God's desire for people to have deep, meaningful relationships with one another as they cared for creation together.

What does the creation story tell you about God's design for community?

_____

_____

When you hear the word "family" what words or thoughts come to your mind?

_____

_____

The best physical environment for people to grow up in is a family. The same is true spiritually. No matter how healthy or unhealthy your natural family is, we all need a spiritual family — a church community — to help us experience transformation.

Look back at the stages of spiritual development from Week 1, Day 1 (*see page 13*). Ideally, families include people in various stages of life. If you're a spiritual child, you need spiritual parents to help you grow. Having other spiritual children to rub shoulders with is a great benefit, too! No matter what stage you're in, interaction with people in other life stages can help you thrive and grow.

Not only do individuals experience transformation through relationships, but nothing else provides an opportunity to practice living according to God's ways quite like living in community. Jesus wanted His disciples to live in unity:

"My prayer is not for them alone. I pray also for those who will believe in me through their message, that all of them may be one, Father, just as you are in me and I am in you. May they also be in us so that the world may believe that you have sent me." — John 17:20-21

God's plan for cultural transformation includes community. As individuals grow, they form healthy families and churches that bring change into the world.

What has your experience with church community been like up to this point?

_____
_____
_____
_____

How do you think God might want to transform your understanding and experience of Christian community?

_____
_____
_____
_____

WEEK 5 / DAY 2 – RECEIVE
GROWING TOGETHER

Use the Scriptures provided to answer the questions below. <u>Underline</u> the basis for your answers in the margin.

EVERY PERSON MADE in the image of God is made for community.

1. What key elements were at play in the first "Jesus community"? (Acts 2:41-47)

_____
_____
_____

This first century church met both in large gatherings ("in the temple courts") and in smaller groups ("in their homes"). We need to be united with a larger church community, but also find a smaller group or team where we can be truly known, cared for, and encouraged. On this kind of team, we can also be mentored, find a place of ministry, and reach out to others.

2. In what other ways did these believers live together? (Acts 4:32-35)

_____
_____

3. What are the benefits when two people walk together instead of walking alone? (Ecclesiastes 4:9-12, see *next page*)

_____
_____
_____

ACTS 2:41-47
⁴¹ Those who accepted his message were baptized, and about three thousand were added to their number that day. ⁴² They devoted themselves to the apostles' teaching and to fellowship, to the breaking of bread and to prayer. ⁴³ Everyone was filled with awe at the many wonders and signs performed by the apostles. ⁴⁴ All the believers were together and had everything in common. ⁴⁵ They sold property and possessions to give to anyone who had need. ⁴⁶ Every day they continued to meet together in the temple courts. They broke bread in their homes and ate together with glad and sincere hearts, ⁴⁷ praising God and enjoying the favor of all the people. And the Lord added to their number daily those who were being saved.

ACTS 4:32-35
³² All the believers were one in heart and mind. No one claimed that any of their possessions was their own, but they shared everything they had. ³³ With great power the apostles continued to testify to the resurrection of the Lord Jesus. And God's grace was so powerfully at work in them all ³⁴ that there were no needy persons among them. For from time to time those who owned land or houses sold them, brought the money from the sales ³⁵ and put it at the apostles' feet, and it was distributed to anyone who had need.

4. What is another result of living in tight community with other believers? (Proverbs 27:17)

5. What else do accountable relationships provide? (Hebrews 10:24-25)

6. What would life be like if you were surrounded by friends who followed the instructions in Hebrews 10:24-25? Give specifics.

In a healthy community, people take ownership for creating their culture. The responsibility of encouraging and building up others lies with each of us, including you!

7. *The Message* translation states Hebrews 10:24 as follows: "Let's see how inventive we can be in encouraging love and helping out..." What are some practical ways you can encourage the closest people around you?

8. In light of these biblical teachings about growing in community, what is the Lord leading you to adjust in your life?

An important feature of community includes accountability. You can check out some great questions to use in small groups in Appendix B and at integratethefaith.com.

ECCLESIASTES 4:9-12
[9] Two are better than one, because they have a good return for their labor: [10] If either of them falls down, one can help the other up. But pity anyone who falls and has no one to help them up. [11] Also, if two lie down together, they will keep warm. But how can one keep warm alone? [12] Though one may be overpowered, two can defend themselves. A cord of three strands is not quickly broken.

PROVERBS 27:17
[17] As iron sharpens iron, so one person sharpens another.

HEBREWS 10:24-25
[24] And let us consider how we may spur one another on toward love and good deeds, [25] not giving up meeting together, as some are in the habit of doing, but encouraging one another—and all the more as you see the Day approaching.

WEEK 5 / DAY 3 – REFLECT & RESPOND
GET IN THE BOAT

IN ORDER TO ACCOMPLISH OUR MISSION to disciple the nations, we must embrace the fact that discipleship is a team sport. When Jesus called His disciples, they not only followed Him, they also joined a team. The following scenario was repeated over and over again:

Immediately Jesus made his disciples get into the boat and go on ahead of him to Bethsaida, while he dismissed the crowd. — Mark 6:45

While others could come and go as they pleased, the disciples had to stay in close quarters with their teammates — no matter how tired they were of each other, and no matter who needed a shower! Their interactions with one another were an essential part of their personal transformation.

Once we're "in the boat," we experience difficulties and come face to face with our teammates' weaknesses and imperfect attitudes. Our differences, preferences, and pride come into play. When we're on mission together, we learn to work through these issues to love and serve others.

Do you have a "boat"? Is there a team of people you're living in close proximity with? Are you part of a small group that loves one another in practical ways and encourages each other toward personal and community transformation? (This could be a church small group, a ministry team, or a group of friends who informally-but-intentionally pursue personal and community transformation together.)

If yes, how is the Lord leading you to value and invest in this group? If not, where could you intentionally seek out this kind of team? (If you don't know, ask God and others in your church. This is a prayer He would love to answer!)

GOING DEEPER

A well-rounded believer has three types of intentional relationships to ensure health, growth, and effective ministry: 1) coaches, 2) peers — close Christian friends, and 3) disciples/potential disciples — people you're reaching out to or helping to grow.

What does your intentional relationship circle look like?

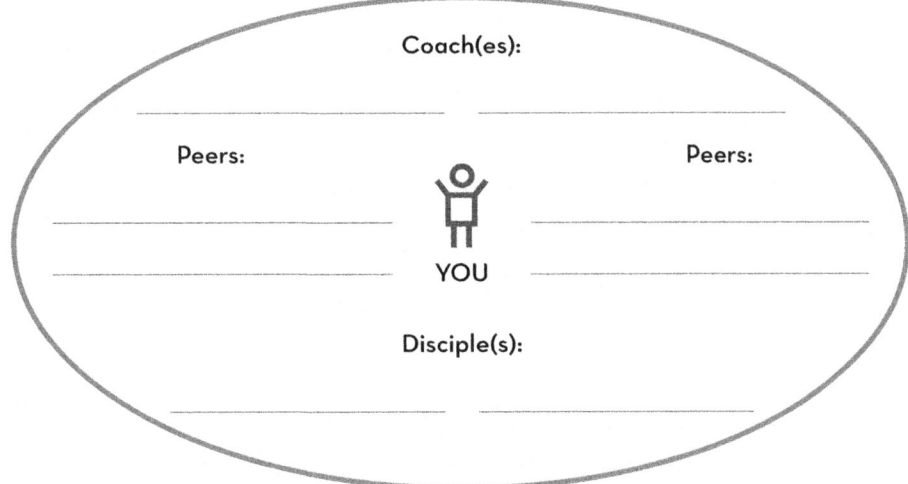

Which of these three relationships categories may require more intentionality?

_____

What will you do about this? (i.e., find and join a small group or ministry team, hold each other accountable, challenge each other to take risks and grow in your faith, invest in someone far from Christ, invite someone new to church or a small group, ask someone from your church to mentor you, etc.) When will you do it?

_____

_____

_____

WEEK 5 / DAY 4 – RECEIVE
WE OVER ME

ROMANS 12:1-16

¹ Therefore, I urge you, brothers and sisters, in view of God's mercy, to offer your bodies as a living sacrifice, holy and pleasing to God—this is your true and proper worship. ² Do not conform to the pattern of this world, but be transformed by the renewing of your mind. Then you will be able to test and approve what God's will is—his good, pleasing and perfect will.

³ For by the grace given me I say to every one of you: Do not think of yourself more highly than you ought, but rather think of yourself with sober judgment, in accordance with the faith God has distributed to each of you. ⁴ For just as each of us has one body with many members, and these members do not all have the same function, ⁵ so in Christ we, though many, form one body, and each member belongs to all the others. ⁶ We have different gifts, according to the grace given to each of us. If your gift is prophesying, then prophesy in accordance with your faith; ⁷ if it is serving, then serve; if it is teaching, then teach; ⁸ if it is to encourage, then give encouragement; if it is giving, then give generously; if it is to lead, do it diligently; if it is to show mercy, do it cheerfully.

⁹ Love must be sincere. Hate what is evil; cling to what is good. ¹⁰ Be devoted to one another in love. Honor one another above yourselves. ¹¹ Never be lacking in zeal, but keep your spiritual fervor, serving the Lord. ¹² Be joyful in hope, patient in affliction, faithful in prayer. ¹³ Share with the Lord's people who are in need. Practice hospitality.

¹⁴ Bless those who persecute you; bless and do not curse. ¹⁵ Rejoice with those who rejoice; mourn with those who mourn. ¹⁶ Live in harmony with one another. Do not be proud, but be willing to associate with people of low position. Do not be conceited.

Use the Scriptures provided to answer the questions below. <u>Underline</u> the basis for your answers in the margin.

LIVING IN COMMUNITY requires a WE over ME mentality. We must live in such a way that we consider others over ourselves, and act in a way that benefits the team.

In Romans 12, Paul writes to believers about how to view themselves and the community. He encourages them to offer themselves as a living sacrifice, holy and pleasing to God. This is much more than an individual pursuit.

1. How does Paul encourage us to think about ourselves? (Romans 12:3-5)

———————————————————————

2. What are some of the spiritual gifts available for the development of the church body? (Romans 12:6-8)

———————————————————————

———————————————————————

3. How can you practically apply the gifts you have to serve other people?

———————————————————————

4. How are followers of Jesus to relate to each other? (Romans 12:9-16)

———————————————————————

Paul implores the Romans to see themselves as an integral part of a larger community that reflects the goodness of God to the world around them.

Living like this isn't easy. It requires a high level of faith, love, and community. One of the challenges is staying encouraged and hopeful. Paul addresses this in his letters to the Colossians and the Thessalonians.

5. What happens when we encourage others? (1 Thessalonians 5:8,11)

_____

_____

6. What are some other attitudes that help build a healthy community? (Colossians 3:12-16)

_____

_____

_____

7. How can you practically show gratitude to God and the people He has placed in your life? (Colossians 3:16)

_____

_____

8. How does Jesus say we should respond to our enemies? (Matthew 5:43-45)

_____

_____

9. Which of the attitudes and actions identified above do you want God to transform during this season of your life? What practical steps can you take to grow in these areas?

_____

_____

_____

Pray for God's grace to work this into your life. And let a friend or two know what you're focusing on so they can pray and encourage you in this process, too.

---

1 THESSALONIANS 5:8, 11
[8] But since we belong to the day, let us be sober, putting on faith and love as a breastplate, and the hope of salvation as a helmet... [11] Therefore encourage one another and build each other up, just as in fact you are doing.

COLOSSIANS 3:12-16
[12] Therefore, as God's chosen people, holy and dearly loved, clothe yourselves with compassion, kindness, humility, gentleness and patience. [13] Bear with each other and forgive one another if any of you has a grievance against someone. Forgive as the Lord forgave you. [14] And over all these virtues put on love, which binds them all together in perfect unity. [15] Let the peace of Christ rule in your hearts, since as members of one body you were called to peace. And be thankful. [16] Let the message of Christ dwell among you richly as you teach and admonish one another with all wisdom through psalms, hymns, and songs from the Spirit, singing to God with gratitude in your hearts.

MATTHEW 5:43-45
[43] "You have heard that it was said, 'Love your neighbor and hate your enemy.' [44] But I tell you, love your enemies and pray for those who persecute you, [45] that you may be children of your Father in heaven. He causes his sun to rise on the evil and the good, and sends rain on the righteous and the unrighteous."

WEEK 5 / DAY 5 – REFLECT & RESPOND
EXTENDING RECONCILIATION

COMMUNITY is not only for those who are already "in." Our mission is to bring transformation to the lives of those who currently seem far from God. Jesus demonstrated an incredible ability to relate with all people. His approach to sinners was radically inclusive, loving, and intentional:

Now the tax collectors and sinners were all gathering around to hear Jesus. But the Pharisees and the teachers of the law muttered, "This man welcomes sinners and eats with them."

Then Jesus told them this parable: "Suppose one of you has a hundred sheep and loses one of them. Doesn't he leave the ninety-nine in the open country and go after the lost sheep until he finds it? And when he finds it, he joyfully puts it on his shoulders and goes home. Then he calls his friends and neighbors together and says, 'Rejoice with me; I have found my lost sheep.' I tell you that in the same way there will be more rejoicing in heaven over one sinner who repents than over ninety-nine righteous persons who do not need to repent. — Luke 15:1-7

What opportunities might you have in your day-to-day life to show grace to people who are far from God?

_____

_____

How can you share your faith in a way that demonstrates God's love and grace?

_____

_____

He said to them, "Go into all the world and preach the gospel to all creation." — Mark 16:15

 GOING DEEPER

When Jesus was on earth, He encountered a group of men who were in it together for one another.

One day Jesus was teaching, and Pharisees and teachers of the law were sitting there. They had come from every village of Galilee and from Judea and Jerusalem. And the power of the Lord was with Jesus to heal the sick. Some men came carrying a paralyzed man on a mat and tried to take him into the house to lay him before Jesus. When they could not find a way to do this because of the crowd, they went up on the roof and lowered him on his mat through the tiles into the middle of the crowd, right in front of Jesus.

When Jesus saw their faith, he said, "Friend, your sins are forgiven."

The Pharisees and the teachers of the law began thinking to themselves, "Who is this fellow who speaks blasphemy? Who can forgive sins but God alone?"

Jesus knew what they were thinking and asked, "Why are you thinking these things in your hearts? Which is easier: to say, 'Your sins are forgiven,' or to say, 'Get up and walk'? But I want you to know that the Son of Man has authority on earth to forgive sins." So he said to the paralyzed man, "I tell you, get up, take your mat and go home." Immediately he stood up in front of them, took what he had been lying on and went home praising God. Everyone was amazed and gave praise to God. They were filled with awe and said, "We have seen remarkable things today." — Luke 5:17-26

What happened to the paralyzed man? What role did his friends play?

_____

_____

The faith of this man's friends led them to take radical action on his behalf — and helped him encounter healing and forgiveness. In the same way, God uses others to bring us to Jesus and He uses us to lead others to Jesus.

Name two or three friends God has placed in your life that need healing:

_____

What are you actively doing to "bring them before Jesus?" (i.e., Bible study, holding each other accountable, challenging each other to take risks and grow in your faith)

_____

_____

Continue to the next page to explore ways for sharing your faith with others.

Consider the following instructions for interacting with people outside the community of believers:

Be wise in the way you act toward outsiders; make the most of every opportunity. Let your conversation be always full of grace, seasoned with salt, so that you may know how to answer everyone. — Colossians 4:5-6

Take some time to prepare how you will share your story of how God is changing you. Use the following prompts to map out your testimony on the next page.

1. Consider your life before knowing God.
2. How did you meet God?
3. How has your life changed?
4. How is that change affecting the world around you?

Your testimony is powerful. It's the story of God's goodness and grace in your life. It is a story worth sharing well. *(Note, you may wish to write a longer version at some point, but remember that sometimes, less is more. Hit the highlights first so your listener has time to digest them and be impacted.)*

But in your hearts revere Christ as Lord. Always be prepared to give an answer to everyone who asks you to give the reason for the hope that you have. But do this with gentleness and respect... — 1 Peter 3:15

Your testimony is one avenue of sharing your faith. This should be combined with communicating the Gospel message. A good way to do this is to tell the four parts of God's story: Creation, Fall, Redemption, and Restoration, as discussed in Kingdom Living 1 (see Appendix F).

Who needs to hear this story? When will you share it with them?

_____

_____

Practice communicating your testimony and the 4-Part Gospel with someone from your small group, or whoever you are going through Kingdom Living 2 with. Then go share it with someone! (Let your friends pray with you and be sure and tell them how it goes.)

YOUR TESTIMONY

WEEK 5 / DAY 6 – RECEIVE
RELATIONSHIP ESSENTIALS

Use the Scriptures provided to answer the questions below. <u>Underline</u> the basis for your answers in the margin.

AS WE ARE SEEING, one of God's primary means to transform us is through our relationships. However, not everyone who interacts with others experiences positive transformation! Certain attitudes and practices are essential.

FORGIVE

1. What is an essential part of experiencing cleansing, forgiveness, and healing from sin? Why do we need to do this with one another? (1 John 1:9, James 5:16, John 20:23)

_____

_____

When you confess your sins, you receive both forgiveness and healing. This keeps your conscience free and helps you overcome sinful habits.

It's our responsibility to quickly confess our sins, both to God and trusted friends. Don't wait for others to ask — come into the light as soon as you realize that you have sinned.

2. What if someone repeatedly sins against us? (Luke 17:3-4)

_____

3. Is unforgiveness an option? Why/why not? (Mat. 6:14-15)

_____

Learning to forgive is a crucial component of following Jesus. Instead of holding onto things that offend us, we must continually forgive each other — just as God forgives us. Forgiving does not excuse the sin, but helps restore harmony.

Harboring unforgiveness is toxic. If there's someone you need to forgive, ask God if simply releasing them in your heart is best, or if you should also go to them in person.

---

1 JOHN 1:9
⁹ If we confess our sins, he is faithful and just and will forgive us our sins and purify us from all unrighteousness.

JAMES 5:16
¹⁶ Therefore confess your sins to each other and pray for each other so that you may be healed. The prayer of a righteous person is powerful and effective.

JOHN 20:23
²³ "If you forgive anyone's sins, their sins are forgiven; if you do not forgive them, they are not forgiven."

LUKE 17:3-4
³ ..."If your brother or sister sins against you, rebuke them; and if they repent, forgive them. ⁴ Even if they sin against you seven times in a day and seven times come back to you saying 'I repent,' you must forgive them."

MATTHEW 6:14-15
¹⁴ "For if you forgive other people when they sin against you, your heavenly Father will also forgive you. ¹⁵ But if you do not forgive others their sins, your Father will not forgive your sins."

PROVERBS 9:8-9
⁸ Do not rebuke mockers or they will hate you; rebuke the wise and they will love you. ⁹ Instruct the wise and they will be wiser still; teach the righteous and they will add to their learning.

BE TEACHABLE

4. What kind of people benefit from the instruction, teaching, and correction of others? What kind of people respond with negativity? (Proverbs 9:8-9, see *previous page*)

_____
_____

5. How are we to approach a fellow believer who falls into sin or wanders from the truth? (James 5:19-20, Galatians 6:1)

_____
_____

6. Is it hard for you to receive input from others? Why/why not?

_____
_____

Openness and teachability often do not come naturally to us — but they are essential to our ongoing transformation.

WORK IT OUT

7. How should we approach tension in a relationship? When? (Matthew 5:23-24)

_____
_____

8. What steps did Jesus tell us to take if a fellow believer sins against us? How do these help build healthy community? (Matthew 18:15-17)

_____
_____
_____

9. Why do you think we should be careful about getting offended? (Proverbs 19:11) What issues are worth addressing? What did Jesus model for us?

_____
_____

JAMES 5:19-20
[19] My brothers and sisters, if one of you should wander from the truth and someone should bring that person back, [20] remember this: Whoever turns a sinner from the error of their way will save them from death and cover over a multitude of sins.

GALATIANS 6:1
[1] Brothers and sisters, if someone is caught in a sin, you who live by the Spirit should restore that person gently. But watch yourselves, or you also may be tempted.

MATTHEW 5:23-24
[23] "Therefore, if you are offering your gift at the altar and there remember that your brother or sister has something against you, [24] leave your gift there in front of the altar. First go and be reconciled to them; then come and offer your gift."

MATTHEW 18:15-17 (ESV)
[15] "If your brother sins against you, go and tell him his fault, between you and him alone. If he listens to you, you have gained your brother [16] But if he does not listen, take one or two others along with you, that every charge may be established by the evidence of two or three witnesses. [17] If he refuses to listen to them, tell it to the church. And if he refuses to listen even to the church, let him be to you as a Gentile and a tax collector."

PROVERBS 19:11 (ESV)
[11] Good sense makes one slow to anger, and it is his glory to overlook an offense.

WEEK 5 / DAY 7 – REST
LOVE IS FROM GOD

WHEN IT COMES TO COMMUNITY, love is paramount. And while it may sometimes feel difficult to love others, the Scriptures show us how this is indeed possible.

Dear friends, let us love one another, for love comes from God. Everyone who loves has been born of God and knows God. Whoever does not love does not know God, because God is love. This is how God showed his love among us: He sent his one and only Son into the world that we might live through him. This is love: not that we loved God, but that he loved us and sent his Son as an atoning sacrifice for our sins. Dear friends, since God so loved us, we also ought to love one another. — 1 John 4:7-11

What stands out to you in this passage about God's love?

_____

_____

_____

It's important to remember that God's love is what transforms us. Our ability to love others comes from first receiving God's love. In a list of the qualities that God's Spirit produces in our lives, love comes first:

But the fruit of the Spirit is love, joy, peace, forbearance, kindness, goodness, faithfulness, gentleness and self-control. Against such things there is no law. Those who belong to Christ Jesus have crucified the flesh with its passions and desires. Since we live by the Spirit, let us keep in step with the Spirit. Let us not become conceited, provoking and envying each other. — Galatians 5:22-26

After we have freely received God's love, we can then choose to freely love others.

Love is patient, love is kind. It does not envy, it does not boast, it is not proud. It does not dishonor others, it is not self-seeking, it is not easily angered, it keeps no record of wrongs. Love does not delight in evil but rejoices with the truth. It always protects, always trusts, always hopes, always perseveres. Love never fails.... And now these three remain: faith, hope and love. But the greatest of these is love. — 1 Corinthians 13:4-8, 13

Name some ways that God is transforming your attitude/lifestyle to reflect His love.

How are you participating in the kind of community expressed in the verses above?

What ways do you see God's love transforming the world around you?

Take some time to reflect on the ways God is bringing you into a greater experience of community. Ask Him to continue this process in you, in your local church, in your city, and in the world.

Write your reflection/prayer here:

APPENDIX

APPENDIX A
DEFINITIONS OF KEY TERMS

ALMS – money or other donations given to the poor and needy.

DISCIPLE (literally a "disciplined learner") – knows and follows Christ, is being changed by Christ, and is committed to the mission of Christ.

FLESH – old thought patterns, habits, and ways of trying to get what we want. God calls us to "crucify our flesh" and replace these old ways with His truth. As we trust Him in these areas, our souls and bodies experience renewal.

IMPUTED RIGHTEOUSNESS – the righteousness of Christ that a believer receives as an immediate gift from God at the moment of justification.

IMPARTED RIGHTEOUSNESS – the gracious work of God over time in a believer's life, as He instills Christ-like character in us through the process of sanctification.

JUSTIFICATION – being declared righteous in the sight of God (think "just as if I'd never sinned"); takes place when we turn from our sins and place our trust in Christ and His work on the cross, receiving a new nature in place of our old sinful nature.

KINGDOM OF GOD – the rule and reign of God. It was inaugurated on earth through the ministry, death, and resurrection of Jesus; is progressively expanding through God's people throughout history; and will be consummated at the second coming of Christ. Thus, the kingdom has come, the kingdom is coming, and the kingdom will come.

OFFERING – gifts to a church, missions endeavor, or other project after our tithe.

SANCTIFICATION – the process of being progressively transformed into the person God intends us to be.

SAVED/SALVATION (Greek: "sozo") – rescued from danger or destruction, delivered from sin and the righteous judgment of God; kept safe and sound; made well, healed, restored to health; preserved when in danger of destruction. We are saved when we first trust in and pledge our allegiance to Christ, we are being saved as we experience progressive transformation/sanctification, and we will be completely saved when Christ returns, our bodies are resurrected and we become "like Him" (1 John 3:2).

SOUL – our minds, emotions, and wills. After Adam and Eve sinned, our souls took the reins of our lives.

SPIRIT – the vitalizing, energizing, empowering agent; it is that essence of the human being that corresponds with God's nature and can commune with God, who is Spirit.

STRONGHOLD – a particular belief or action that we strongly defend which gives our enemy a grip in our life, to the detriment of our spiritual growth. Composed of thoughts, attitudes, and beliefs that do not reflect the character of God.

TITHE – the first 10% of our income, given to God.

APPENDIX B
THE REJECTION CYCLE

FEELING REJECTED

Rejection can take many different forms. You could feel rejected when people say or do unkind things to you. You could feel rejected when someone you care about ignores or overlooks you. Another painful type of rejection is feeling judged or condemned by others. Rejection can be intentional or unintentional, real or perceived. Regardless of the type of rejection, the result is often that we feel unloved, unappreciated, or unwanted.

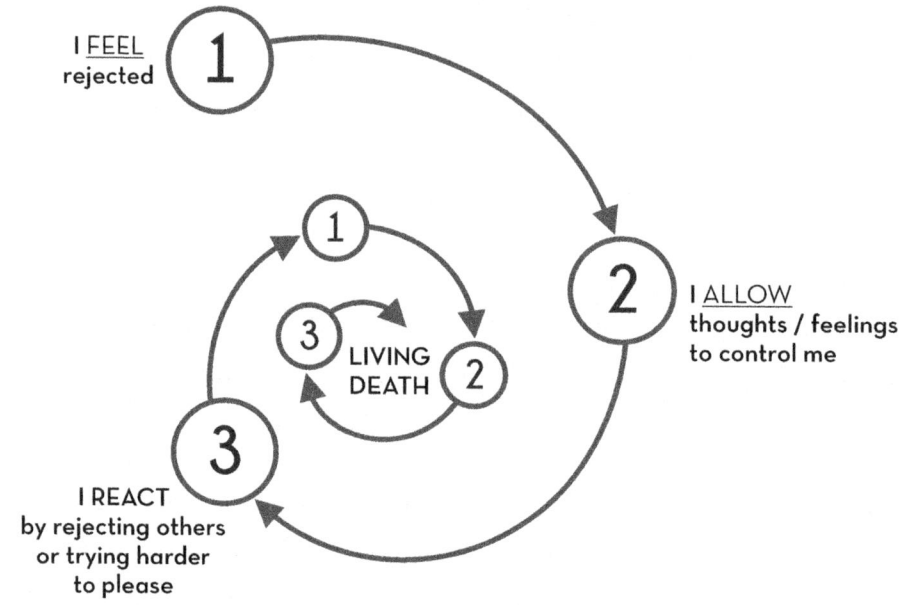

APPENDIX

OUR CHOICE

When feeling rejected, you have a choice: 1) allow the negative thoughts and feelings to control your reaction and continue in the downward spiral, or 2) believe what GOD says about you and respond based on your value and identity as a beloved son or daughter of the Most High God. You might be amazed to find how this perspective helps you extend love and forgiveness, even to the very people who may have triggered the feelings of rejection.

REVERSING THE REJECTION CYCLE

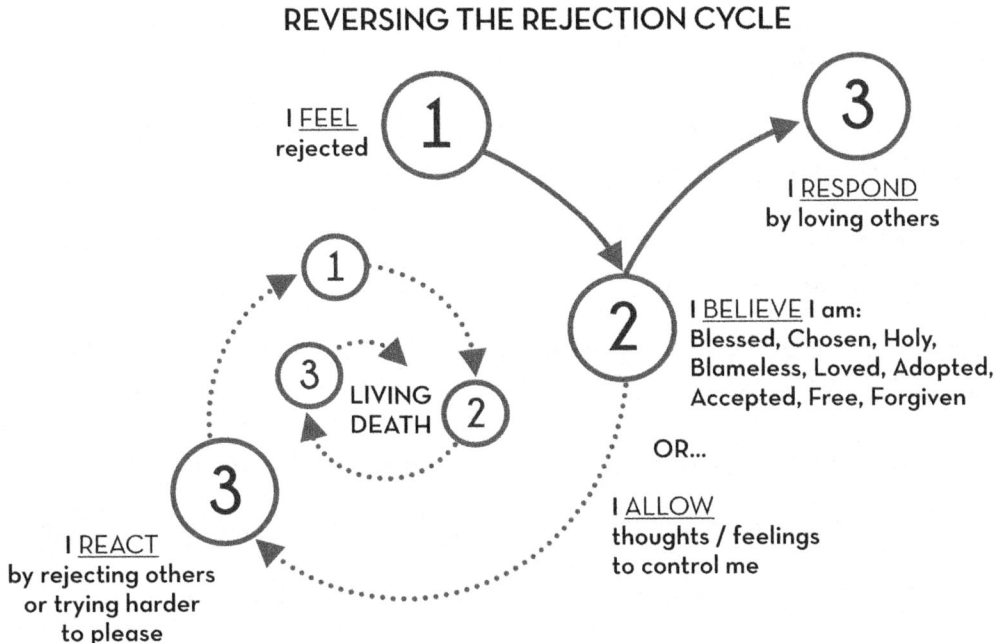

APPENDIX C
ACCOUNTABILITY QUESTIONS (FROM NEIL COLE)

RELATIONSHIPS are essential to encourage us and spur us forward in the process of transformation. The following accountability questions can be helpful as we seek to partner with the Holy Spirit's work in transforming our lives, and our relationships.

- Have you been a testimony this week to the greatness of Jesus Christ with both your words and actions?

- Have you been exposed to sexually alluring material or allowed your mind to entertain inappropriate thoughts about someone who is not your spouse this week?

- Have you lacked any integrity in your financial dealings this week, or coveted something that does not belong to you?

- Have you been honoring, understanding, and generous in your important relationships this past week?

- Have you damaged another person by your words, either behind their back or face-to-face?

- Have you given in to an addictive behavior this week? Explain.

- Have you continued to remain angry toward someone else?

- Have you secretly wished for another's misfortune so that you might excel?

- Did you finish your reading this week and hear from the Lord? What are you going to do about it?

- Have you been completely honest with me?

APPENDIX

Use the space below to write a few personal accountability questions.
Ask the Holy Spirit to highlight areas of opportunity for growth or refinement, then share these questions with a friend to help keep you accountable.

APPENDIX D
FAITH & FINANCES

"...those of you who do not give up everything you have cannot be my disciples." — Luke 14:33

THE BIBLE has more than 2,300 verses about managing money, resources and assets. To follow Christ and live with faith we must trust and honor God with our money. As Jesus said:

"For where your treasure is, there your heart will be also." — Matthew 6:21

GIVING BECOMES MUCH EASIER when we recognize that all we have actually belongs to God, and we are only managers. God does not own a portion of our lives or money, but everything.

The earth is the LORD's, and everything in it, the world, and all who live in it... — Psalm 24:1

THREE TYPES OF FINANCIAL GIVING (see definitions in Appendix A)

1. Tithes   2. Offerings   3. Alms

Religion that God our Father accepts as pure and faultless is this: to look after orphans and widows in their distress and to keep oneself from being polluted by the world. — James 1:27

WHAT IS A TITHE?

1. "Tithe" literally means "tenth." A tithe is 10% of our income.

"A tithe of everything from the land, whether grain from the soil or fruit from the trees, belongs to the LORD; it is holy to the LORD.... Every tithe of the herd and flock—every tenth animal that passes under the shepherd's rod—will be holy to the LORD." — Leviticus 27:30,32

2. A tithe is the first part of our income. We "pay God first."

Honor the Lord with your wealth, with the first fruits of all your crops. — Proverbs 3:9

"I the LORD do not change... Return to me, and I will return to you," says the LORD Almighty. "But you ask, 'How are we to return?' Will a mere mortal rob God? Yet you rob me. But you ask, 'How are we robbing you?' In tithes and offerings. You are under a curse—your whole nation—because you are robbing me. Bring the whole tithe into the storehouse, that there may be food in my house. Test me in this," says the LORD Almighty, "and see if I will not throw open the floodgates of heaven and pour out so much blessing that there will not be room enough to store it. I will prevent pests from devouring your crops, and the vines in your fields will not drop their fruit before it is ripe," says the LORD Almighty. "Then all the nations will call you blessed, for yours will be a delightful land," says the LORD Almighty. — Malachi 3:6-12

WHY GIVE?

1. Because God commanded us to do so.

Be sure to set aside a tenth of all that your fields produce each year. — Deuteronomy 14:22

"Do not think that I have come to abolish the Law or the Prophets; I have not come to abolish them but to fulfill them." — Matthew 5:17

2. To fund the Kingdom.

"Bring the whole tithe into the storehouse, that there may be food in my house." — Malachi 3:10

"The Lord's work requires the Lord's tithe, and gifts and offerings over and above the tithe. Nothing better reveals commitment than giving. No commitment means no giving, and little commitment means token giving." — RJ Rushdooney

3. To open the door of God's abundant provision.

Tithing helps us break free from the materialism that is so prevalent in our culture. (A smaller percentage of American Christians tithe today than during the Great Depression!) It also helps bring us into a place of living according to God's economics, instead of being limited by our own resources and natural abilities.

"Give, and it will be given to you. A good measure, pressed down, shaken together and running over, will be poured into your lap. For with the measure you use, it will be measured to you." — Luke 6:38

Remember this: Whoever sows sparingly will also reap sparingly, and whoever sows generously will also reap generously. Each of you should give what you have decided in your heart to give, not reluctantly or under compulsion, for God loves a cheerful giver. And God is able to bless you abundantly, so that in all things at all times, having all that you need, you will abound in every good work. Now he who supplies seed to the sower and bread for food will also supply and increase your store of seed and will enlarge the harvest of your righteousness. You will be enriched in every way so that you can be generous on every occasion, and through us your generosity will result in thanksgiving to God.
— 2 Corinthians 9:6-11

APPENDIX E
DECLARATIONS TO GROW YOUR FAITH

WHO I AM IN CHRIST

Apart from Jesus Christ, I can do nothing; but in Jesus Christ I can do all things, so I can bring glory to Him. Therefore, I see myself as He sees me according to His living Word, for my life is hidden with Christ in God. I will train myself to say the same things as God says in His Word, for how can two walk together except they be agreed?

Through regular time in His presence, I will cultivate a sensitivity to hearing His voice. He will make His Word a reality in my life as I nurture my friendship with Him. Faith will not be a formula or technique in my life, but the natural byproduct of knowing Him intimately as my faithful Lord. Knowing Him, I can totally trust Him. His Word will always be the final authority in my life. I base my entire life upon him and His living Word. Because I meditate upon His word day and night and carefully do all that is written in it, my way shall be prosperous.

I will be a success to the glory of God. All His blessings shall come upon me and overtake me because I obey the voice of the Lord, my God. Of this I am confident: Those who seek the Lord shall not lack any good thing. I will not live by bread alone, but by every word that proceeds out of the mouth of God.

VICTORY

I'm not just an ordinary man or woman; I'm a son/daughter of the living God. I'm not just a person; I'm an heir of God, and a joint heir with Jesus Christ. I'm not just an old sinner; I'm a new creation in Jesus, my Lord. I'm part of a chosen generation, a royal priesthood, a holy nation; I'm one of God's people. I'm not under guilt or condemnation. I refuse discouragement, for it is not of God. God is the God of all encouragement. There is therefore now no condemnation for those in Christ Jesus. Satan is a liar. I will not listen to his accusations. I gird up the loins of my mind. I am cleansed in the blood. No weapon formed against me shall prosper, and I shall confute every tongue rising against me in judgment. My mind is being renewed by the Word of God. I pull down strongholds; I cast down imaginations; I bring every thought captive to the obedience of Christ.

I am accepted in the beloved. If God be for me, who can be against me? Greater is He that is in me than he that is in the world. Nothing can separate me from the love of Christ. As the Father loves Jesus, so Jesus loves me. I'm the righteousness of God in Christ. I'm not a slave of sin; I'm a slave of God and a slave of righteousness. I continue in His Word; I know the truth, and the truth has set me free. Because the Son sets me free, I am free indeed. He who is born of God keeps me, and therefore the evil one does not touch me. I've been delivered out of the kingdom of darkness. I'm now part of the kingdom of God. I don't have to serve sin anymore. Sin has no dominion over me.

I will not believe the enemy's lies. He will not intimidate me. He is a liar and the father of lies. Satan is defeated. For this purpose the Son of God came into the world, to destroy the works of the devil. No longer will he oppress me. Surely oppression makes a wise man mad. I will get mad at the devil. I defeat him by the blood of the Lamb, by the word of my testimony, not loving my life even to death. I will submit to God. I will resist the devil and he will flee. No temptation will overtake me that is not common to man. God is faithful; He will not let me be tempted beyond my strength, but with the temptation will also provide the way of escape that I may be able to endure. I will stand fast in the liberty with which Christ has made me free. Where the Spirit of the Lord is, there is liberty. The law of the Spirit of Life in Christ Jesus has set me free from the law of sin and death. Christ always causes me to triumph. I'll reign as a king in life through Christ Jesus. As a young man/woman I am strong, the Word of God abides in me, and I have overcome the evil one. I am more than a conqueror through Christ who loves me. I am an overcomer. I can do all things through Christ who strengthens me. Thanks be to God who gives me the victory through Jesus Christ, my Lord!

FAITH

I can do all things through Christ who strengthens me. By my God I can run through a troop and leap over a wall! He makes my feet like hind's feet; He makes me walk upon high places. With man this is impossible; but with God all things are possible! All things are possible to him who believes. If I have faith the size of a grain of mustard seed, I can say to a mountain, "Move," and it will move, and nothing will be impossible to me. I'm a believer; I'm not a doubter. I know that whatever is not of faith is sin. I know that without faith it is impossible to please God. I know I am to live by faith, and if I shrink back the Lord has no pleasure in me.

Every person is given a measure of faith; I'll develop my faith to the glory of God. I have faith towards God. My faith is not in my faith, but in a living God who said He would never fail or forsake me. Therefore I choose to walk by faith and not by sight. I trust in the Lord with all my heart and don't lean to my own understanding. I'm not ruled by my feelings. I'm not in bondage to my emotions. I'm not under the circumstances; I'm above the circumstances. I'm seated with Christ in heavenly places. The steps of a righteous man are ordered by the Lord. Many are the afflictions of the righteous, but the Lord delivers them out of them all. The righteous man falls seven times, but rises again. Champions don't give up; they get up. One thing I do, forgetting what lies behind, straining forward to what lies ahead, I press on toward the goal for the prize of the upward call of God in Christ Jesus, my Lord. I put my hand to the plow, and I don't look back. I run to win. Zeal for Your house consumes me. The kingdom of heaven comes by violence, and those who take it, take it by force. It's not by might, nor by power, but by His Spirit. He ever lives to make intercession for me. He is able to do exceedingly far more abundantly above all that I even dare think or ask, by the power of work at within me. He who began a good work in me will bring it to completion in the day of my Lord Jesus. Boldly, I can approach the throne of grace to receive mercy and grace for help in the time of need. I'll be anxious for nothing. He will keep me in perfect peace for my mind is stayed on Him.

Therefore I enter His rest. I've been crucified with Christ, nevertheless I live, and the life I now live, I live by faith in the Son of God who loved me and gave Himself for me. Whatever is born of God overcomes the world. This is the victory that overcomes the world, even my faith. I choose this day to live by faith, to walk by faith, to see through the eye of faith. Therefore, I am an overcomer. I'm going from faith to faith, strength to strength, glory to glory. The path of the righteous is like the light of dawn, which shines brighter until the full day!

BOLDNESS

I give no opportunity to the devil. I give no place to fear in my life. That which man fears comes upon him. Fear hath torment. The fear of man brings a snare, but perfect love casts out fear. I sought the Lord, and He heard me and delivered me from all my fears. God has not given me a spirit of fear, but a spirit of love, power and a sound mind. In righteousness I am established, so I'll be far from oppression. I will not fear or be in terror. It shall not come near me. The Lord is my light and salvation. Whom shall I fear? The Lord is the strength of my life; of whom shall I be afraid? God is my refuge and strength, a very present help in trouble.

Therefore I will not fear. If I were still trying to please men, I should not be a servant of Jesus Christ. But I am a servant of the Most High God. I fear not, for He is with me. I'll not be dismayed, for He is my God. He will strengthen me; He will help me; He will uphold me with His victorious right hand. I am not ashamed of the gospel for it is the power of God unto salvation to those who believe. I'm a minister of reconciliation. I'm an ambassador for Jesus Christ. The anointing I've received abides in me. The anointing breaks every yoke. I received power when the Holy Spirit came upon me to be His witness. His Word which comes out of this mouth will not return void, but will accomplish His purpose and prosper in the thing for which it was sent. I know my God; I am strong; I will do exploits. As He is, so am I in this world. I am righteous, therefore, I am bold as a lion. He will never fail me or forsake me; therefore, I can boldly say, "The Lord is my helper; I'll not be afraid." What can man do to me? As a young man/woman, I am strong. The Word of God abides in me. I have overcome the evil one. I am an overcomer. Greater is he that is in me than he that is in the world. I am complete in Him. I am more than a conqueror through Christ who loves me. Grant, Lord, to Your servant to speak Your Word with all boldness while You stretch out Your hand to heal and signs and wonders are performed through the name of Your holy servant, Jesus!

HEALTH

I will bless the Lord with all my heart, for He not only forgives my sins, He heals all diseases. Because the Lord is my Refuge, the Most High, my habitation, no evil shall befall me, no plague will come near my dwelling place. He gives His angels charge over me to guard me in all my ways. It's His will that I prosper and be in health, even as my soul prospers. Jesus went about doing good and healing all who were oppressed by the devil. He said, "I'll remove sickness from the midst of you." He is the Lord, my healer, Jesus my loving Lord. My body is for the Lord, and the Lord is for my body. He bore away my sickness and carried away my diseases and by His stripes, I was healed. The Son of Righteousness shall rise with healing in His wings. The same spirit that raised Jesus from the dead is at work in my mortal body, giving me life. I expect a miracle. Jesus Christ is the same yesterday, today and forever. Is anything too hard for the Lord?

For all things are possible to him who believes. I am not just a hearer of the Word, I'm a doer of the Word. Therefore, I am blessed in my doing, for faith without action is dead. I will not only confess the Word, but I will be a doer of the word.

JOY

I renounce a spirit of heaviness and put on the garment of praise so that He may be glorified. I will bless the Lord at all times; His praise shall continually be in my mouth. The joy of the Lord is my strength. Jesus bore my grief.

This is the day that the Lord has made. I will rejoice and be glad in it. I rejoice with joy unspeakable and full of glory. I rejoice in the Lord always. I do all things without grumbling and complaining. His words were found, and I ate them, and they became unto me a joy and delight to my heart. In spite of trials, I offer sacrifices of joy. I will sing, yes, I will sing praise to the Lord. I have the high praises of God in my mouth and a two-edged sword in hand. I have set the Lord always before me. Because He is at my right hand, I shall not be moved. Therefore, my heart is glad and my soul rejoices. My body also dwells secure. You show me the path of life. At Your right hand are pleasures forevermore. I will rejoice in the Lord; I will rejoice in the God of my salvation.

I wait upon the Lord, and He renews my strength. I will mount up with wings like eagles; I will run and not be weary; I will walk and not faint.

PROSPERITY

I continue to keep my way of life free from the love of money; I cannot serve God and money. All things come from Thee and of Thine own I have given Thee. Being faithful with money, I am entrusted with true riches. I do not rob God in my tithes and offerings, therefore, I'm not cursed with a curse and the devourer is rebuked. I put the Lord to the test, and the Lord opens the windows of heaven and pours down an overflowing blessing.

I do not grow weary in doing good, for in due season I will reap because I do not lose heart. I cast my bread upon the waters, and I find it after many days. One person gives freely yet grows all the richer; another withholds what he/she should give and only suffers want. The generous person will prosper and one who waters he/she. I've been young and now I am old, yet I've not seen the righteous forsaken or their children begging bread. I am ever giving liberally and lending, and my children become a blessing. My God supplies all my needs according to His riches in glory in Christ Jesus. I give and it is given to me, good measure, pressed down, shaken together, running over me, men pour into my lap. If I sow sparingly, then I will also reap sparingly. So I will sow bountifully, and therefore, reap bountifully. God loves a cheerful giver.

He is able to provide me with every blessing in abundance so I may always have enough of everything in order to provide in abundance for every good work. He who supplies seed to the sower and bread for food will supply and multiply my resources and increase the harvest of my righteousness.

I do not see godliness as a means of selfish gain. My passion is to see the gospel of the kingdom preached throughout the whole world as a testimony to all the nations; then the end will come. I do all I can to hasten the coming of the day!

DESTINY

The eyes of the Lord run to and fro throughout the whole earth in order to show Himself strong on behalf of those whose hearts are fully blameless toward Him. God rewards those who diligently seek Him. He who calls me is faithful, and He will do it. I'm not lukewarm. I'm not a compromiser. I'll not be conformed to this world. I'm not a loser; I'm a winner. I'm a partaker of His divine nature. God indwells my body. I run the race to win. His power is made perfect in weakness.

When the enemy comes in like a flood, the Spirit of the Lord will raise up a standard. I'm part of that standard. We are the soldiers of the army of salvation that God is raising up to save the world. I'll not despise the day of small beginnings. We will reclaim that which the thief has stolen through tradition and ignorance. The earth is the Lord's and the fullness thereof, the world and all who dwell therein. He said He would pour out His Spirit in these last days, sons and daughters would prophecy; young men and women would see visions; old men and women would dream dreams. I'm part of this end-time vision, for without it, I will perish.

For still the vision awaits its time; it hastens to the end; it will not fail. If is seems slow I will wait for it. It will surely come. It will not delay. Therefore, I have a sense of destiny. Jesus is restoring His church. He is coming back for a glorious church without spot or wrinkle or blemish or any such thing. It will be a triumphant church. It will kick in the gates of hell. I'm part of this end-time move. I'll pay the price. I'm giving my utmost for His highest. I press on toward the goal for the prize of the high call of God in Christ Jesus, my Lord. I'm out to change my generation. I'm beginning today. I redeem the time. I'm not weighed down by the cares of this life. I cast my cares on the Lord. Whatever the task this day, I'll do it heartily as serving the Lord. I'll pursue excellence, for I serve a God of excellence. I stir up the gifts within me. I'll step out in faith. I'll move in the supernatural. I'll set the captives free.

The Spirit of the Lord is upon me. He has anointed me to preach good news to the poor. He has sent me to proclaim release to the captives, recovery of sight to the blind, to set at liberty those who are oppressed, to bind up the broken-hearted, and to proclaim the acceptable year of the Lord.

I'll not limit the Holy One of Israel. I'll not be disobedient to the heavenly vision. The kingdoms of this world shall become the kingdoms of our God and of His Christ!

APPENDIX F
THE FOUR PARTS OF GOD'S STORY

1	2	3	4
CREATION	FALL	REDEMPTION	RESTORATION
God saw all that he had made, and it was very good… — Genesis 1:31	For the creation was subjected to frustration… in hope that the creation itself will be liberated… — Romans 8:20-21	In him we have redemption through his blood, the forgiveness of sins, in accordance with the riches of God's grace… — Ephesians 1:7	He who was seated on the throne said, "I am making everything new!" — Revelation 21:5

Write a brief description of how you would share the Good News with someone, using the four parts of God's Story as a guide.

_____
_____
_____
_____
_____
_____
_____
_____
_____
_____

APPENDIX

Made in the USA
Monee, IL
02 September 2019